A BENN STUDY · DRAMA

THE NEW MERMAIDS

The Plain Dealer

The Plain Dealer

WILLIAM WYCHERLEY

Edited by
JAMES L. SMITH
Lecturer in English
University of Southampton

LONDON/ERNEST BENN LIMITED

NEW YORK/W. W. NORTON AND COMPANY INC

First published in this form 1979
by Ernest Benn Limited
25 New Street Square, Fleet Street, London EC4A 3JA
& Sovereign Way, Tonbridge, Kent TN9 1RW

© *Ernest Benn Limited 1979*

Published in the United States of America by
W. W. Norton and Company Inc.
500 Fifth Avenue, New York, N.Y. 10036

Distributed in Canada by
The General Publishing Company Limited, Toronto

Printed in Great Britain by
The Bowering Press Ltd, Plymouth and London

British Library Cataloguing in Publication Data

Wycherley, William
  The plain dealer. – (New mermaids).
  1. Title   2. Smith, James Leslie
  3. Series
   822'.4   PR3774.P5

ISBN 0–510–33503–9
ISBN 0–393–90042–8 (U.S.A.)

FOR

E. G. M.

CONTENTS

ACKNOWLEDGEMENTS

THE TEXT AND NOTES to the present edition are indebted to the work
of four earlier editors: to Montague Summers, *The Complete Works
of William Wycherley*, 4 vols. (1924); to George B. Churchill, *The
Country Wife* and *The Plain Dealer* (Boston, 1924); to Gerald
Weales, *The Complete Plays of William Wycherley* (New York,
1966); and to Leo Hughes, *The Plain Dealer* (1967). My introduction
has drawn upon the work of all those critics mentioned in the list
of 'Further Reading' on p. xxxiv; specific acknowledgements are
recognized in the footnotes, but I cannot hope to have included
everyone. I am indebted to the Bodleian Library, Oxford, for per-
mission to reproduce the title-page of the first quarto on p. 1, to the
National Portrait Gallery, London, for the Lely portrait of Wycherley
reproduced as a frontispiece, and to the Trustees of the British
Library, London, for the Gravelot engraving of Westminster Hall
reproduced on pp. 78–9.

Many colleagues at Southampton have been kind enough to
answer my enquiries, but I am especially indebted to Robert Grime,
who took me through Jerry's lawsuit about Fitz, Pere, and Ayle, and
John Swannell, who generously placed at my disposal all the material
he had collected while preparing the Revels Plays edition of *The
Country Wife*. To all, my thanks.

J.L.S.

Sansomes Farmhouse,
Whiteparish.
February, 1979.

INTRODUCTION

THE AUTHOR

ALTHOUGH THE EXACT DATE is unknown, William Wycherley was most probably born on 28 May 1641, the eldest son of a Shropshire royalist whose estate at Clive, some 6 miles north of Shrewsbury, yielded about £600 a year. At fifteen or sixteen he was sent to study in France, and at Angoulême was admitted to the *précieux* salon of the beautiful and brilliant Madame de Montausier, Voiture's correspondent; here he polished his manners, absorbed contemporary French culture, and became a Catholic. William returned to England in the last days of the Protectorate, and entered the Inner Temple on 10 November 1659; some time in July 1660 he went up to Oxford as a gentleman commoner of Queen's College, but stayed there only long enough to become a Protestant again, and left without matriculating.

Over the next decade, legal studies competed for William's time with soldiering and authorship, and came off a poor third. His verses '*On a* SEA FIGHT, *which the Author was in, betwixt the* English and Dutch' suggest he saw service in the second Dutch War (1665–67), but they are not precise enough to identify any particular engagement. His first published work was *Hero and Leander in Burlesque*, a long poem in heroic couplets which appeared anonymously in 1669. *Love in a Wood*, his first comedy, was acted some time during March 1671, and published in quarto the same year; its popular success put Wycherley at once among the wits of the town:

> His Company was not only courted by the Men, but his Person was as well received by the LADIES; and as K. *CHARLES* was extremely *Fond* of him upon account of his *Wit*, some of the Royal Mistresses . . . set *no less Value* upon *Those Parts* in him, of which they were more *proper Judges.*[1]

One such lady was the Duchess of Cleveland, whose influential friendship with Wycherley, if we may believe John Dennis, began romantically enough:

---

[1] Richardson Pack, 'Some memoirs of Mr Wycherley's life', prefixed to Wycherley's *Posthumous Works*, ed. Lewis Theobald (1728), p. 8.

As Mr. *Wycherley* was going thro' *Pall-mall* towards St. *James*'s in his Chariot, he met the foresaid Lady in hers, who, thrusting half her Body out of the Chariot, cry'd out aloud to him, *You*, Wycherley, *you are a Son of a Whore*, at the same time laughing aloud and heartily.[2]

Wycherley was understandably surprised, but when he realized her abuse was in fact a complimentary reference to a song in the play, he turned about, overtook the lady, and replied:

Madam, you have been pleased to bestow a Title on me which generally belongs to the Fortunate. Will your Ladyship be at the Play to Night? Well, she reply'd, *what if I am there? Why then I will be there to wait on your Ladyship, tho' I disappoint a very fine Woman who has made me an Assignation. So,* said she, *you are sure to disappoint a Woman who has favour'd you for one who has not. Yes,* he reply'd, *if she who has not favour'd me is the finer Woman of the two. But he who will be constant to your Ladyship, till he can find a finer Woman, is sure to die your Captive.* The Lady blush'd, and bade her Coachman drive away . . . In short, she was that Night in the first Row of the King's Box in *Drury Lane,* and Mr. *Wycherley* in the Pit under her, where he entertained her during the whole Play.

(Dennis, p. 410)

Their intimacy aroused the jealousy of the Duke of Buckingham, whom the lady had refused, and in revenge he published the name of his successful rival. Wycherley feared the King's anger, but friends arranged a meeting at which the dramatist's wit so charmed the Duke that he became his patron and in 1672 made Wycherley one of his equerries and a Captain in his own regiment. *Love in a Wood* had been presented by the King's Company at their Theatre Royal in Bridges Street, but when this theatre was burned down in January 1672, Wycherley was obliged to offer his next play to the rival company at the Duke's Theatre in Dorset Garden. *The Gentleman Dancing-Master* was played there on 6 February 1672, but according to the prompter it was 'like't but indifferently' and laid aside after only six performances.[3] For his third play, Wycherley returned to the King's Company, now established in their new Theatre Royal in Drury Lane. *The Country Wife* was given here, probably for the first time, on 12 January 1675, and its success was followed by that of *The Plain Dealer*, which was presented by the same company at the same theatre on 11 December 1676. Wycherley was now called 'The Plain Dealer' by his friends, praised as a satirist by Dryden,

---

[2] John Dennis, Letter to Richardson Pack dated 1 September 1720, in *The Critical Works of John Dennis*, ed. Edward Niles Hooker, 2 vols. (Baltimore, 1939–43), II, 409.

[3] John Downes, *Roscius Anglicanus* (1708), p. 32.

and courted by the King. When he fell sick of a fever in 1678, Charles honoured his lodgings with a visit, prescribed a winter in the south of France, and undertook to provide him with £500 for expenses. Wycherley obediently wintered in Montpellier, and on his return to England in the spring of 1679 was appointed tutor to the King's bastard son the Duke of Richmond, at a promised salary of £1,500 a year. But Charles was a king whose word no man relied on, and all the tutor received, according to Pope, was 'now and then a hundred pound—not often'.[4]

This same year, Wycherley visited Tunbridge Wells, perhaps to take the waters. As he paused at a bookseller's there, in came

> my Lady *Drogheda*, a young Widow, rich, noble, and beautiful . . . and enquir'd for *the Plain Dealer. Madam*, says Mr. *Fairbeard, since you are for the* Plain Dealer, *there he is for you*, pushing Mr. *Wycherley* towards her. *Yes*, says Mr. *Wycherley, this Lady can bear plain Dealing, for she appears to be so accomplish'd, that what would be Compliment said to others, spoke to her would be plain Dealing. No, truly, Sir*, said the Lady, *I am not without my Faults any more than the rest of my Sex, and yet notwithstanding all my Faults, I love plain Dealing, and never am more fond of it than when it tells me of my Faults. Then, Madam*, said Mr. *Fairbeard, you and the* Plain Dealer *seem design'd by Heaven for each other*. (Dennis, p. 411)

They married the same year, without informing the King. When the news broke, Charles was stung by Wycherley's presumed ingratitude and revoked the tutorship. The Lady, too, proved another embarrassment, for

> she could not endure that he should be one Moment out of her Sight. Their Lodgings were in *Bow-street, Covent-Garden*, over-against the *Cock*, whither if he at any time went with his Friends, he was oblig'd to leave the Windows open, that the Lady might see there was no Woman in Company, or she would be immediately in a downright raving Condition. (Dennis, p. 412)

Worse was to follow, for when she died and left him her fortune in 1681, her family disputed the will and Wycherley was forced into ruinous litigation which soon landed him in Fleet Prison for debt. Pack tells us

> that the *Bookseller* who Printed his *PLAIN-DEALER*, by which he got almost as much *Money* as the *Author* gained *Reputation*, was so *Ungrateful* to his Benefactor, as to refuse to lend him *Twenty Pounds* in his *extreme Necessities*. (p. 10)

---

[4] Joseph Spence. *Observations, Anecdotes, and Characters of Books and Men*, ed. James M. Osborn, 2 vols. (Oxford, 1966), I, 35.

But help came, unexpectedly, from the Court; on 14 December 1685 a friend contrived to have *The Plain Dealer* performed before James II, who

> was so Charmed with the *Entertainment,* that he gave immediate Orders for the *Payment* of his DEBTS, adding to *That Grace* a PENSION also of 200 *l. per Annum,* while he continued in *ENG-LAND.* (Pack, p. 10)

When James fled the country in 1688, Wycherley lost the pension and retired to Clive. On his father's death in 1697 he inherited the estate on a life tenancy and returned to London, where he presided over a new generation of wits from his chair at Will's Coffee House in Bow Street, a short step from his old rooms opposite 'The Cock'. The *Miscellany Poems* of 1704, published at his own expense, added nothing to his reputation. His memory deteriorated ever more rapidly, and he allowed his remaining papers to be corrected for the press by the young Alexander Pope, who rewrote some lines, inserted a great many of his own, but found the rest so incoherent and repetitious he advised Wycherley to transform them into prose maxims. This material eventually appeared in the *Posthumous Works* of 1728, to which Pope added a second volume the next year containing his own carefully edited correspondence with the dramatist.

Wycherley's last years were marked by ill-health, failing faculties, poverty, and peevishness. On his deathbed he married again, Pope supposed to discharge his debts and disinherit a troublesome nephew, who was thus obliged to pay the young widow a pension of £400 a year.[5] The nephew objected and went to law, claiming the marriage was forced upon Wycherley by his cousin Thomas Shrimpton, the groom was half conscious and the bride Shrimpton's secret mistress. He lost the case, but three months later Shrimpton married the rich young widow. William Wycherley died on the last day of 1715, the victim of a savage plot worthy of his own comedies. He was buried in St Paul's, Covent Garden, alongside Kynaston, who created Freeman in *The Plain Dealer*, and Peter Lely, whose portrait of Wycherley hangs in the National Portrait Gallery.

[5] Pope to Edward Blount, 21 January 1715/16, in *The Correspondence of Alexander Pope,* ed. George Sherburn, 5 vols. (Oxford, 1956), I, 328–9; the nephew's case is presented in Howard P. Vincent's 'The death of William Wycherley', *Harvard Studies and Notes in Philology and Literature,* XV (1933), 219–42.

THE PLAY

As long as Men are False and Women Vain,
While Gold continues to be Virtues Bane,
In pointed Satyr *Wycherley* shall reign.
(John Evelyn)

The Plain Dealer is a comedy of no manners which attacks the double-dealing codes of Wycherley's society in all their varied guises; in the supercilious forms and slavish ceremonies of a Lord Plausible, whose empty compliments debase the currency in which true merit should be paid; in the malicious gossip of a school for scandal which dissects with tender care the failings of their absent friends; and even in the perversion of that great plain dealer, justice, at Westminster Hall, where barristers unite to cheat the courts with splutter, eloquence, or tedium, and solicitors throw up a long-standing client's brief from pique or to pursue the favour of a lord. Nor are the theatres themselves exempted from this universal vice, for when the talk turns to the hideous obscenity of Wycherley's last play, the audience is jolted sharply out of that complacent unawareness with which the victims of a satire most usually view their portraits in the glass. What *should* a modest woman do when told a dirty joke in public? If she blushes, turns aside, or hides her face behind a fan, she is demonstrating not her modesty but a self-conscious prudishness. The prurient relish with which Olivia then gloats over every clandestine obscenity in the play must make audiences at *The Plain Dealer* squirm with embarrassment; at such a moment there will surely be more brilliant acting in the auditorium than on the stage. The theatre is as full of hypocrites as Westminster Hall, but at every public gathering, even at Whitehall or the Court, the story is the same: the entire social structure is corrupt:

here you see a bishop bowing low to a gaudy atheist; a judge to a door-keeper; a great lord to a fishmonger, or a scrivener with a jack-chain about his neck; a lawyer to a serjeant at arms; a velvet physician to a threadbare chemist; and a supple gentleman-usher to a surly beef-eater; and so [they] tread round in a preposterous huddle of ceremony to each other, whilst they can hardly hold their solemn false countenances. (I. 297–304)

The speaker here is Captain Manly, the plain dealer of our title, and he is addressing his lieutenant, Freeman. Both are hard up; both are sailors, and to some extent therefore remain outsiders from another element on land; and both are clearly men of sense; they join together, for example, in the ridicule of fops who think that railing is satire, talking a mark of wit, and breaking windows humour. But when they look at the moral chaos all around them, their reactions differ. Manly lashes out at knaves and stands on his integrity, while Freeman laughs at fools and is prepared to profit from them. They debate their relative positions in the first act of the play. Manly says he would expose a courtier who promises more than he performs, a lawyer who takes bribes, an officer who proves a coward, a titled poet who lacks talent, or a prude who sleeps with her chaplain. Such honesty is no doubt admirable, but Freeman is quick to point out it is not a sure way to success in the world. And when Manly claims his moral superiority is also more effective on pragmatic grounds as well, Freeman is tersely unconvinced:

> Well, doctors differ. You are for plain dealing, I find; but against your particular notions I have the practice of the whole world.
> (I. 291–3)

This debate between the unyielding moral absolutes of Manly and the easy-going cynicism of his lieutenant is continued intermittently throughout the play, and articulated still more forcefully in the plots they weave.

Freeman's lively chase after the Widow Blackacre's jointure is conducted with more regard to fun and energy than ethics. His merry nature is established by the sailors' talk before his first appearance, and his first line declares an easy tolerance of fools who feed his laughter. Like Horner in *The Country Wife*, he is a totally amoral rake who uses his intelligence to penetrate the varied pretences of the world around him, and by pretending in his turn manipulates them to his own advantage. But Horner is a man of means whose only business is his pleasure; Freeman is without a sou and must use the promise of his sexual prowess to buy financial independence. He will marry the widow for her fortune, if he can, and promises to drudge faithfully and earn his wages. The first hurdle is a rival suitor in the superannuated shape of Major Oldfox, but the lady sends him packing as a feeble, paralytic, impotent, fumbling, frigid nicompoop, and later on he succeeds only in ravishing her through the ears with his acrostics. Freeman's second hurdle is more obstinate, for a married woman cannot go to law, and litigation is the widow's only pleasure. Battle is joined when he buys the favour of her booby son and through him steals her legal papers with a view to blackmail. But by claiming Jerry is a bastard the widow manages to evade his clutches, and it is only when Freeman strikes out on a new offensive by having her arrested that she is forced to sign the peace upon his terms, and he is lavishly rewarded with a handsome settlement without the need to drudge for it. Clearly, there is a deal of sprightly impudence in this head-on collision between two worldly cynics both well endowed with wit and cunning, but there is a kind of comic justice too. The widow is a venomous old harridan who follows law like the professionals, for profit more than justice; she is willing to lay out a hundred pounds to purchase an illegal suit in champerty, and spends part of the last act fabricating seals and signatures with some professional false witnesses who have already forged her some six bonds, four deeds, three wills, and her husband's last deed of gift, quite apart from committing half a dozen perjuries in court on her behalf. Moreover, she is beaten at her own game—not one trick left—and this is not because she is dishonest but because she is less cunning in her legal double-dealing than an amateur like Freeman; he is too good a joker to have any law in his head, but he knows where it can be purchased from the law-pimps of Whitefriars. Thus the widow is defeated by the very code she lives by, and Freeman triumphs by judicious use of that same amoral mother wit by which he lives.

To make this comic justice yet more perfect, Freeman's victory carries in its train the liberation of that chopping minor, young Squire Jerry. It is, in its small way, another judgement on the side of natural fertility. The widow is a powerful emblem of repression in the play. She lives by choice in poverty, rejects a lusty suitor to pursue the law, and involves herself in cases turning on executors and wills. By her meanness, Jerry is forced to follow in her footsteps, literally, wearing a long black gown and loaded down with green bags holding all her legal documents. He has no pocket money to buy toys, is stuffed with legal textbooks when his thoughts incline to soldiering, adventure, or the playhouse, and is as totally a prisoner of his mother's monomania as Freeman would be if he married her. She is their common enemy. Like Margery in *The Country Wife*, Jerry is persuaded to exchange an old, harsh, turn-key guardian for another who will give his sexual drives their head. And when Freeman secures his own financial independence, he negotiates good terms for his pawn and ally too. Young Jerry now will have free access to the maid-servants' bedrooms, and a settled annuity of some forty pounds a year to spend on all the pleasures of the town. He ends the play without his gown, in Freeman's old red breeches, as much a 'man of myself' as Freeman is a free man. Comedy, said Donatus, expresses the view that life should be embraced.

Yet doubts, however small, remain. On his own terms, Freeman is successful; but he is twice outwitted by the widow. A true rake-hero is not shown at such a disadvantage. Moreover, his considerable gifts of personality and intelligence might have encouraged him to aim a little higher than the humiliation of a grotesque old harpy who is a mere volume of shrivelled blurred parchments and the law. Again, his cynicism is no doubt justified by events, and integrity is, as he says, as useless 'to a man that would thrive in the world as square play to a cheat or true love to a whore' (I. 245–6); yet these comparisons, which he accepts so cheerfully, must surely make him look a little cheap. And finally, of course, there is the whole question of Eliza. She functions on the fringes of the play as Olivia's companion and Wycherley's mouthpiece in the second act debate about *The Country Wife*. Yet her intelligence and knowledge of the town are strikingly like Freeman's, and his last speech almost echoes something she had said much earlier: 'the world is but a constant keeping gallant, whom we fail not to quarrel with when anything crosses us, yet cannot part with't for our hearts' (II. 10–12). It would be absurd to say an audience expects these two sensible and sympathetic people to meet and fall in love, for we do not spend the interval match-making through the cast-list, and after all they never actually exchange a word, or even share the stage before the final scene. Yet these two characters do marry in the last scene of *Le Misanthrope*, which served as Wycherley's source for *The Plain Dealer*, and he had introduced a similar 'ideal' pairing in the Harcourt and Alithea relationship in *The Country Wife*. His refusal to do so here may mean he does not wish to set up either Freeman or Eliza as a standard by which others may be judged.

The doubts surrounding Manly in the main plot of the play are much more serious. Indeed, his very nature is in question. Some readers find him perfect, a superb *beau idéal*, an outstanding pillar of virtue, even Wycherley's own spokesman or perhaps an idealized portrait of his friend the Earl of Mulgrave. Others have dismissed him as a psychopath, a monomaniac, a fool whose conduct is not far removed from that of a madman, a warped idealist like Alceste in *Le Misanthrope*, a churlish kill-joy like Malvolio or Jaques in *As You Like It*, a disillusioned malcontent like Marston's Malevole, a satirist who is afflicted with the vices he attacks in others, a rakish hero, a ferocious sensualist, a romantic lover, a surly dupe, a stupid butt, or a richly comic 'humours' character like Morose in *The Silent Woman*.[6] Although they seem so contradictory, there is an element

---

[6] For Manly as Musgrave, see J. M. Auffret, '*The Man of Mode* and *The Plain Dealer*: common origin and parallels', *Etudes Anglaises*, XIX (1966), 209; for Manly's other roles, see D. F. Haskell's unpublished thesis, 'The role of the hero in the comedies of William Wycherley' (Brown, 1970), pp. 103–45.

of truth in most of these descriptions, and more than an element in some.

For example, Manly is clearly written in the 'humours' mode made popular by Jonson, and Shadwell's praise of his 'new humour' in the Prologue to *Bury Fair* (1689) shows that Wycherley's contemporaries thought so too. That Shadwell thought his humour 'new' is rather odd, though, for Manly shares his surly honesty with the manly Colonel Blunt in Howard's *The Committee* (1662) and the yet more brutal Manly in D'Urfey's *Madam Fickle* (1676); behind all of them is the Theophrastan character of 'A Blunt Man' included in John Earle's *Microcosmographie* (1628). Like him, Manly 'is a great enemy to the fine gentlemen, and these things of compliment, and hates ceremony in conversation, as the Puritan in religion. He distinguishes not betwixt fair and double dealing, and suspects all smoothness for the dress of knavery. He starts at the encounter of a salutation . . . is exceedingly in love with his humour . . . for he must speak his mind'.[7] And so on, for another paragraph. One novelty with Manly is that Wycherley has placed him at the centre of the play, unlike his early 'humours'—men like Don Diego, Paris, Gripe—who are always left as cameos to decorate the sub-plots. Another is that Wycherley combines two 'humours' here by making his blunt man a sailor. Manly is probably too much the gentleman to speak their strange sea-dialect, and his language lacks the salty metaphors which make Ben in Congreve's *Love for Love* so richly comic. But the seamen who attend him bring a strong whiff of the briny with them in their forecastle jests and talk of wooden legs and Biscay storms, and on the stage his weather-beaten features, wide-kneed breeches, greasy sword belt, and tarpaulin brandenberg would emphasize his kinship with them. All this careful naval background adds contour and colour to a flat convention, but as Pepys explains it also helps to show why Manly is so much at sea on land :

> The sea can never be a trade for a nobleman or courtier, because it is impossible for him to live so in it, but that his conversation and company and diet and clothes and all must be common with the meanest seaman, and his greatest trust too, while his other companions of his own sort are but troubles to him and no use. Nor can he be neat and nice to make love in the fashion, when he comes among the ladies.[8]

[7] Reprinted in *A Book of Characters*, ed. Richard Aldington (n.d.), pp. 234–5; for a fuller description, see Alexander H. Chorney, 'Wycherley's Manly reinterpreted', *Essays Critical and Historical Dedicated to Lily B. Campbell* (Berkeley and Los Angeles, 1950), pp. 161–9.

[8] *The Tangier Papers of Samuel Pepys*, ed. Edwin Chappell, Publications of The Navy Records Society, LXXIII (1935), p. 166; for sailors' dialect, see William Matthews, 'Sailors' pronunciation in the second half of the

Moreover, it is Manly's sea-life which provides him with a standard of comparison to judge this neat, nice, fashionable world. The sea, at least, is honest. There is nothing hypocritical about fair weather or a hurricane, and every passing ship is quickly recognized as friend or foe. Moral judgements can be made in black and white. And when a ship's crew fights against a storm or picaroon, each member knows that he will sink or swim with all the rest. The sea breeds courage, loyalty, and generous self-sacrifice as well. The voyage itself is taking Manly to bask in an alternative society on the sunny side of the globe, a world of downright barbarity, it seems, where widows are required to share their husband's funeral pyre and men devour each other with the ferocity of hungry lions and tigers. Like the sea, the Indies threatens death at every turn, but like the sea it also breeds men with the qualities to meet that threat unflinching. Manly and his sailors bring these virtues with them when they land. The sailors cheerfully admit they can deny a woman nothing since they are so newly come on shore—an idea Freeman repeats to the widow—and no doubt Black Kate at Wapping satisfies their needs with that same absence of hypocrisy the play's Epistle Dedicatory commends in a noted London procuress. They defend Captain Manly's London stair-well as if they were guarding the scuttle of a powder-room, and he rewards them with his last twenty pounds because he would not 'have the poor, honest, brave fellows want' (III. 744–5).

Sea-going loyalty, generosity, honesty, and courage, then, are Manly's great criteria, and since the world around him is so signally devoid of all these virtues, he lashes out at it with the surly vigour of a 'humorous' blunt man. It cannot be denied that these attacks are brilliant, witty, passionate, and widely ranging over every kind of fraud in social life and personal relations. Many of these diatribes, which make up a good proportion of the play, reflect opinions Wycherley expressed elsewhere in non-dramatic writings. Some of the *Miscellany Poems* of 1704 read like Manly; 'To the Universal FRIEND' attacks another Plausible, and 'To my Lord Chancellour Boyle' deals with legal malpractice; a third is called '*Upon the* Injustice *of the* Law: *A* SATYR', and a fourth 'The World Unmask'd. *A* SATYR: *Against all Vain Pretenders, their Hypocrisie, Affectation, and Vanity; which generally make Men disappoint their own Ends, by their own Desires*'. Such poems have encouraged readers to assume that Manly speaks for Wycherley himself, an idea

---

seventeenth century', *Anglia,* LIX (1935), 193–251; I am indebted for both references to A. C. P. Messenger's unpublished thesis, 'The comedy of William Wycherley' (Cornell, 1964).

he began by signing the Epistle Dedicatory of the play as 'The Plain Dealer'. Dryden, Dennis, Congreve, Pope, and other friends all called him 'Manly' or 'Plain Dealer' Wycherley in print, Mr Fairbeard introduced him to his future wife as the 'Plain Dealer', and Lansdowne tells us he was distinguished 'by the unanimous Consent of his Contemporaries' with 'the just Appellation of Manly *Wycherley*'.[9] Clearly, these titles are intended to be complimentary, and it must follow that to those who used them Manly was an admirable, sympathetic man. Other evidence, however, shows that such a view is over-simple. Lansdowne's tribute to the manly satirist also points out the gentle, inoffensive disposition of the man, and Pack's brief memoir makes the paradox more plain:

> His PLAYS are an Excellent *Satire* upon the *Vices* and *Follies* of the Age in which he lived. His STYLE is *Masculine,* and his WIT is *Pointed*: And yet with all that *Severity* and *Sharpness* with which he appears on the STAGE, they who were of his *Familiar Acquaintance* applauded him for the *Generosity* and *Gentleness* of *his* MANNERS. He was certainly a Good-natured Man. (p. 9)

When Wycherley was writing *The Plain Dealer* he was still a fashionable rake, and the satiric poems of the *Miscellany* share the sheets with other verses which reflect more libertine preoccupations. There is '*A* SONG *against Delays in* LOVE', another '*To a* LADY, *who wore Drawers in an Ill Hour*', and a third is comprehensively entitled '*Upon a* Lady's Fall *over a* Stile, *gotten by running from Her* Lover; *by which She show'd Her* Fair Back-side, *which was Her best Side, and made Him more Her Pursuer than He was before*'. What would Manly make of that? There is, of course, no fundamental contradiction here. Rochester combined the roles of moralist and rake in his own life and writings, and Wycherley explores the same duality in his plays. In this sense *The Plain Dealer* is the flip side of *The Country Wife,* since each takes for hero an exaggerated aspect of his own nature. In fact, each play has both, for Horner's sexual triumph is contrasted with the moral eminence of Harcourt and Alithea as Manly's moral eminence is contrasted with the libertine success of Freeman. A lesser dramatist might be content with plot and sub-plot counterpointing such contrasted values, but Wycherley digs deeper yet. He makes each spokesman humanly imperfect, as inconsistent and as fallible as life itself. Freeman has limitations, even when we judge him by his own modest standards; Manly's code is nobler, and its problems more complex.

To begin with small things. Manly is an awkward cuss, a bearish

[9] George Granville, Baron Lansdowne, *A Character of Mr Wycherley and his writings* (1718), p. 26.

kill-joy who admits he cannot laugh, finds no delight in fools, and will not stay to see the grotesque spectacle of Jerry dressed in the remains of Freeman's shipwrecked wardrobe. And surely there is something dangerously extremist about a man who has his front door guarded by two servants with drawn cutlasses, just to keep unwanted visitors away. More seriously, his idealism is self-destructive, even suicidal. He sinks his ship to stop her falling into the hands of profiteers, and by doing so destroys a national asset, half his personal estate, all his sailors' savings, and Black Kate's small venture too; honour can be bought too dear. Again, his fury lacks proportion. He spends the same fierce indignation on a venal lawyer and a comparatively harmless fop; surely taking bribes is far more serious a vice than Plausible's unhappy halitosis. He lacks discrimination too. When a sailor rescues him from drowning or an alderman suggests a mutually profitable swindle, he rewards them both with blows about the head. In fact, he is extremely unperceptive, and never more so than when he prides himself on his acute perception of intrinsic worth. He says his heart admits of but one friendship and one love. Waiting patiently to fill these roles are Freeman and Fidelia, the one a true friend who has seen active service by his side, the other a loyal and loving girl who has disguised herself in man's clothes to join his ship as a young volunteer. (We are not to ask how she got on below decks.) But Manly dismisses Freeman as a latitudinarian in friendship, that is, no friend, and Fidelia as a milksop and a flattering, lying coward. Instead, he puts his trust in Vernish and Olivia, who turn out to have married secretly and tricked him out of his remaining fortune; his bosom friend is a remorseless, treacherous, lecherous double-dealer and his one true love an affected, prudish, greedy, vain, deceitful, money-grubbing nymphomaniac. She encouraged Manly's love by pretending to hate the world as much as he did, and he trusted her because he thought he could not be deceived. The criticisms here are varied, but none suggest plain dealing in itself is less than admirable, although its spokesman may, at times, lack both proportion and discrimination in his onslaughts. All the remaining points are those a Freeman might have made: plain-dealing men are grumpy, anti-social, difficult to live with, poor, naïf, and credulous, an easy prey to villains who can impose upon their virtue for a mean advantage. The basic trouble, then, with Manly's code is that the world will not accommodate it. The fault is with the world and not with him.

The play does more than hold up to our scrutiny the complex, contradicting attitudes that surround the ideal of plain dealing. It flings Manly head first into the intriguing world, and waits to see if

he will sink or swim. It could be argued he does both. He discovers
the true nature of Olivia, detests himself for still desiring her, sends
Fidelia to pimp for him, and when the lecherous Olivia sets up an
assignation with the young volunteer, Manly replaces her in Olivia's
bed, contrives a second meeting to expose her villainy, gets his jewels
back, unmasks both Fidelia and Vernish, and instead of setting off
at once for the Indies, settles down to marriage with Fidelia, who
is, of course, really a rich heiress newly come to her estate.

Such an astonishing intrigue can be interpreted in many ways. It
has been argued, for example, that Manly here degenerates pro-
gressively until he has reneged on all his principles.[10] He forces poor
Fidelia to beg, pimp, lie, deceive, and flatter, is guilty of hypocrisy
or self-deception when he calls his lust an honourable vengeance, and
finally surrenders to a ferocious pleasure which makes him as
contemptible as Olivia herself. The trouble with this view is that the
play will not support it. There is no moral criticism made of Manly
for his act; indeed, he is rewarded at the final curtain with jewels, a
friend, a bride, her fortune, and the admiration of all the decent
standers-by. Comic dramatists do not usually hand out such substantial jack-pots to characters they want us to disapprove of. Nor would
Wycherley's friends have called him Manly if they thought the name
stood for an unprincipled degenerate. A second view relates the plot
to other Restoration comedies where clever men can even verge on
promiscuity without prejudicing an audience against them.[11] Dori-
mant in *The Man of Mode* wooes, beds, and then rejects Bellinda,
but is still allowed to make a profitable marriage with a nice girl at
the end. Indeed, many such heroes only have a well-planned seduc-
tion to commend them to an audience. This argument would be
more persuasive if Freeman were in question here, not Manly. Nor
can the bed-trick be dismissed as a neutral stock device, a mechan-
ism of the plot quite innocent of moral value, unless, of course, we
think that Wycherley would be prepared to scuttle his play for a few
dirty jokes and an ingenious intrigue. A more satisfactory inter-
pretation of the bed-trick might begin by setting it in the context of
Manly's whole relationship with Olivia. She is a glass where all men
see their faces. Manly looks, and falls in love with his own image:

---

[10] See Rose A. Zimbardo, *Wycherley's Drama: a Link in the Development
of English Satire* (1965), pp. 86–7; Mrs Zimbardo heightens her case
against Manly's honesty by supposing he does not lie with Olivia, and
that his boast to Vernish in V. ii, 123 is therefore 'an act of gratuitous
hypocrisy' (p. 87).
[11] See Katharine M. Rogers, 'Fatal inconsistency: Wycherley and *The
Plain-Dealer*', *A Journal of English Literary History*, XXVIII (1961),
154.

she seems all truth, and hates the lying, masking, daubing world as much as he does. When she betrays him, it is as though he had destroyed himself, a drowned Narcissus. His idealism was the more intense because the world around them was so vile, and now, in their great quarrel scene in the second act, he lashes out in impotent and angry curses, while she replies with only one—the curse of loving on. It is fulfilled. Our sympathy for a decent man destroyed by heartlessness and greed grows into an alarmed concern as Manly drives himself almost to madness, loving her perfect beauty, loathing her moral ugliness, and despising himself for feeling such emotions:

> Damned, damned woman, that could be so false and infamous! And damned, damned heart of mine, that cannot yet be false, though so infamous! . . . Her love! A whore's, a witch's love!—But what, did she not kiss well, sir? I'm sure I thought her lips—but I must not think of 'em more; but yet they are such I could still kiss, grow to— and then tear off with my teeth, grind 'em into mammocks, and spit 'em into her cuckold's face. (IV. i, 103–5, 112–17)

The tortured intensity of feeling here demands a strong response: we pity Manly, understand his cruel revenge and appreciate its psychological 'rightness'. It savours nobly, and since Olivia has clearly put herself beyond the moral pale, it even has a kind of heroic justice. The speech of course reminds a modern reader of Othello's 'I will chop her into messes' (IV. i, 196), and the reminiscence is caught up again when Manly speaks of goats and monkeys (IV. ii, 217) and once more when, like Othello in the brothel scene, he offers payment to Olivia as a common whore (V. iii, 123). But it is probable that Wycherley's own audience related Manly's whole revenge to the heroic dramas of their own day. Arthur Kirsch has argued that there is no reason to suppose a Restoration audience had two different sets of moral standards, one for contemporary comedy and another for heroic plays, and J. H. Wilson has pointed out Manly's unmistakable resemblance to that typical heroic hero, Almanzor in Dryden's *The Conquest of Granada* (1670/71), a role created by Charles Hart, who was Wycherley's first Manly. Almanzor is also rough and blunt, a rugged individualist, fiercely intolerant of cowards, hypocrites, and courtiers, a man whose soul is of such primitive purity that ordinary ethics have no meaning for him:

> Vast is his Courage; boundless is his mind,
> Rough as a storm, and humorous as wind. . . .
> What in another Vanity would seem,
> Appears but noble Confidence in him.
> No haughty boasting; but a manly pride:
> A Soul too fiery, and too great to guide:

He moves excentrique, like a wandring star;
Whose Motion's just, though 'tis not regular.[12]

This could be Manly, even down to the imagery of storms and stars.
Among Almanzor's eccentric motions, however, is a raging passion
for the chaste and lovely Almahide; he prowls outside her chamber
door at night, and is only most reluctantly persuaded not to possess
her before Dryden has had time to marry them in the last act. In such
good company, Manly has no need to defend his moral character;
his heroic aberration is a sign of the noble constancy of his love.

Fidelia remains a problem, though. Her name may echo Imogen's
disguise as the boy Fidele in *Cymbeline*, but her dramatic function
is clearly based on Viola in *Twelfth Night*. Both heroines attend the
man they love in male disguise, both are sent as proxy wooers to a
lady named Olivia, and both find themselves their masters' rivals in
her heart. This pedigree makes Fidelia very difficult to take. She
speaks 'romantic' blank-verse soliloquies, and even her prose style is
liberally endowed with agonized exclamations, protests, cries, and an
apparently inexhaustible allowance of emotive abstract nouns like
love and courage, fear, honour, hope, and death. She seems a pallid,
insubstantial figure, 'literary' and essentially unreal, a symbol, pure
and simple, of devoted love, whose humiliating role as Manly's pimp
involves her in so much misery that our admiration for Manly must
be called in question. While he makes love to Olivia, Fidelia weeps
quietly outside the bedroom door; his success is qualified by her
obvious distress. It is important, therefore, to recall the comic nature
of the role, which would be much more apparent on the stage than
in the study. Imogen and Viola were played by boys, but Fidelia was
created by Elizabeth Boutell, a favourite of the town, whose bright,
long hair and lovely legs made her a perfect choice for 'breeches'
parts like this; she created more than twelve of them, and no doubt
played many more. Her first line in the play, when she says she
loves Manly better than any man can, sets the comic tone; before
the scene is out she promises to 'die' for him, and the sexual joke is
all the funnier to an audience because Manly does not see it. The
tantalizing and misleading way she tells him of her meeting with
Olivia fills the first scene of the fourth act with richly comic
ambiguities, which reach a climax when Manly innocently kisses his
'dear volunteer'. And in the bedroom scenes which follow, where
the dangers of an over-sentimental response are most acute,
Wycherley takes care to fling Fidelia into epicene predicaments which

[12] John Dryden, *The Conquest of Granada*, pp. 9, 58, cited in Arthur
C. Kirsch, *Dryden's Heroic Drama* (Princeton, 1965), pp. 106–7; for
Almanzor and Manly compared, see John Harold Wilson, *A Preface to
Restoration Drama* (Boston, 1965), p. 161.

border upon farce. Olivia first smothers her in kisses then pursues her round the room, pulls her bedwards, and then goes in with Manly by mistake. Fidelia's brief weep is followed by another scene of lecherous evasion. Fidelia feigns epilepsy, rushes out, and then returns at once with Vernish on her tail. Now comes a threatened duel, which she averts by declaring her true sex, but Vernish 'pulls off her peruke and feels her breasts' and instantly resolves on rape. A servant's entry promises a rescue, but when he too turns about and helps his master lock her in the bedroom ('You have a short reprieve'), she has to get away by shinning down the curtains to the street. The speed and pacing of the action here are splendid; every possible permutation of the cast is deftly woven into a continuous intrigue, and every expectation of escape or rape is rapidly reversed with a bewildering and yet inevitable logic. But the real triumph of the scene is that most of it is presumed to take place in total darkness, with the theatre fully lit throughout and the actors pretending to be in the dark. And modern audiences at Peter Shaffer's play *Black Comedy* (1965), which is written in the same convention, show just how funny this can be. Although her romantic role is written in a style that emphasizes all the pain she suffers, there is no danger that she will win easy tears at the expense of Manly's heartlessness. Indeed, Manly himself refutes the charge with a modest apology when he discovers her identity in the final scene:

> The sense of my rough, hard, and ill usage of you, *though chiefly your own fault*, gives me more pain now 'tis over than you had when you suffered it. (V. iii, 106–8, my italics)

And Fidelia thinks herself well rewarded when she rewards Manly with her fortune and her love.

This whole dénouement is the cause of much unease. It is, of course, quite right and proper Vernish and Olivia should be punished for their treachery with poverty, public exposure, and the curse of marriage; like the disloyal, predatory fools of Wycherley's first play, they deserve each other, like mates with like. Manly and Fidelia deserve each other too. Both seek to love an absolute integrity, and both find it only slightly vulnerable to the corruption of this fallen world. Manly's indiscriminate plain dealing is counterpointed here by the slight wound Fidelia received from Vernish in the final scuffle. True, their marriage has an element of conscious, comic artifice, as miraculously bland as Portia's discovery, in the last moments of *The Merchant of Venice*, that Antonio has three rich argosies just come to harbour, and it might be argued that what is acceptable in romantic comedy is out of place in a contemporary comedy of manners. 'Plain dealing is a jewel', says the proverb, 'but they that use it, die beggars'.[13] But Fidelia goes some way to bridge the gap, and Wycherley boldly leaps the rest by reminding his audience in the Prologue that a play can offer better justice than the world at large:

> And where else but on stages do we see
> Truth pleasing, or rewarded honesty? (46–7)

Manly's decision to renounce the Indies for London and Fidelia is carefully prepared for too. The shame of 'loving on' has made him hide his feelings for Olivia from Freeman, and at the beginning of the third act he confesses in soliloquy how hard it is to be a hypocrite. Left to his own devices in Westminster Hall, Manly quickly draws upon himself three quarrels and two lawsuits and perhaps a duel too. Since life imprisonment and forfeiture of all one's goods awaited any man who struck another in the Hall while the courts were sitting, Manly needs a fast, non-violent way to rid himself of fools. Instead of kicking them, he uses his intelligence to probe their weaknesses. Oldfox hurries off when Manly praises a new military drill, and when he asks Novel to act as second in a duel, or a grasping lawyer to accept a pauper's brief, or a greedy alderman to underwrite his credit, they all melt away as well. With the alderman, in fact, Manly at first forgets himself and tweaks his nose, but even this does not deter the man from claiming his society and friendship. Thus Manly discovers that a little social guile is not just a temporary substitute for kicks, but actually more efficient too. A man who has successfully completed such a course of elementary social reconditioning clearly has no need to spurn the world; but it must remain an open question how far such conduct clouds the absolute integrity which Manly showed in the first act. Is it a moral sell-out, the beginning of a landslide? A temporary compromise? Or has Manly simply made that little move from absolute to relative which every adolescent takes in growing up? The play ends with our questions still hanging in the air, for when Manly says that Freeman will suppose it is Fidelia's estate which reconciled him to the world, Freeman agrees, and Manly takes him warmly by the hand, calls him a plain dealer, and at last accepts him as a friend.

With Manly as with Freeman, then, some doubts remain. How is an honest man to live in a dishonest world? Wycherley is too complex a dramatist to offer easy answers, and even in the epigraph he seems to point both ways. 'Jesting often cuts hard knots more forcefully and effectively than gravity'. This might be championing Freeman's way over that of Manly. But it might also be a reference to

---

[13] John Ray, *A Collection of English Proverbs* (1670), p. 132.

Manly's own development. Between severity and ridicule, as Dryden saw, the power of every comedy resides:

> satire lashes vice into reformation, and humour represents folly so as to render it ridiculous. Many of our present writers are eminent in both these kinds; and particularly the author of the *Plain Dealer*, whom I am proud to call my friend, has obliged all honest and virtuous men by one of the most bold, most general, and most useful satires which has ever been presented on the English theatre.[14]

STAGE HISTORY

Despite Dryden's eulogy, the English theatre has never taken *The Plain Dealer* to its heart. The first known performance was given at Drury Lane on 11 December 1676, with the full strength of a brilliant company. Manly was played by Charles Hart, a majestic actor who excelled in Brutus and Othello; the beautiful Elizabeth Boutell played Fidelia; Freeman was Edward Kynaston, a handsome light comedian; and Katherine Corey, a famous Doll Common in *The Alchemist*, played opposite him as the Widow Blackacre. All four had appeared in the first production of *The Country Wife*, as Horner, Margery, Harcourt and Lucy. Also in that production were William Cartwright, who created Oldfox and Sir Jasper Fidget, Mary Knepp, Pepys's pretty friend, who first played Eliza and Lady Fidget, and the eccentric comedian Joseph Haines, who created Lord Plausible and Sparkish. Despite their efforts, the first performances did not take until a claque of Wycherley's friends helped them along. As Dennis tells us,

> There was Villers Duke of Buckingham, Wilmot Earl of Rochester, the late Earl of Dorsett, the Earl of Mulgrave who was afterwards Duke of Buckinghamshire, Mr Savil, Mr Buckley, Sir John Denham, Mr Waller &c . . . when upon the first representations of the *Plain Dealer*, the Town, as The Authour has often told me, appeard Doubtfull what Judgment to Form of it; the foremention'd gentlemen by their loud aprobation of it, gave it both a sudden and a lasting reputation. (II, 277)

It was repeated on 13 December 1676, revived at Oxford for Charles II on 21 March 1681 and at Whitehall before James II on 14 December 1685. The players thought it of sufficient drawing power to choose it for a benefit performance on 2 June 1698. During the first half of the eighteenth century, the play achieved some sixty-six

[14] John Dryden, 'The author's apology for heroic poetry' prefixed to *The State of Innocence* (1677), in *John Dryden: Of Dramatic Poesy and other Critical Essays*, ed. George Watson, 2 vols. (London, 1962), I, 199.

performances, and exercised the talents of Quin in Manly and that rising low comedian Macklin in Jerry Blackacre (14 January 1738). The last performance of Wycherley's play for almost two hundred years was given at Covent Garden on 24 January 1743. A drastic revision of the play by Isaac Bickerstaff, no mean comic dramatist, was given under Garrick's management at Drury Lane on 7 December 1765 and repeated sixteen times before the end of the season. The published text is a grotesquely emasculated travesty of Wycherley's play. In the preface, Bickerstaff boasted he had pruned the play of its 'enormous length, and excessive obscenity'; Manly was too rough, and the fops

> did not seem to me so well contrasted as they might be, while the other comic personages degenerated sometimes into very low farce; neither did I think the part of Fidelia so amiable, or the situations arising from her disguise, quite so amusing, as they were capable of being rendered by a little retouching.[15]

As *The Dramatic Censor* tartly commented, this little retouching 'rendered the play more chaste, but not more entertaining'.[16] Manly never gets to play a scene in Olivia's bedroom, Fidelia is preserved from acting as his pander, and Freeman pursues the Widow to recover an estate which is already his by law. Act Three is divided up into three scenes, beginning with 'a view of Saint James's Park', then changing to Westminster Hall for the Widow and her lawyers, and then changing again to 'the gate of Westminster-Hall' for her meeting with Manly. With these embellishments, the adaptation achieved a respectable success, and ran to forty-nine performances over the years, until a revision by John Philip Kemble laid *The Plain Dealer* in its coffin. Kemble restored some of Wycherley's own dialogue which Bickerstaff had cut, cast himself as Manly, Barrymore as Vernish, and the irresistible Mrs Jordan as Fidelia. The production opened at Drury Lane on 27 February 1796, was repeated on 1 March, and given a last performance on 6 April. There have been no public performances since that time, and only two private ones: one was given by 'The Renaissance Theatre' at the Scala Theatre in London on 15 November 1925, the other in a 'much shortened version' as the second half of a double bill played by students of the one-year overseas course of the London Academy of Music and Dramatic Art, on 9 July 1975.

---

[15] [Isaac Bickerstaff], *The Plain Dealer . . . with alterations from Wycherly* (1766), p. vi.
[16] Cited in Emmett L. Avery, '*The Plain Dealer* in the eighteenth century', *Research Studies of the State College of Washington,* XI (1943), 246, n; I am indebted to this study throughout this section on stage history.

NOTE ON THE TEXT

The Plain Dealer was licensed on 9 January 1676/7, entered in the Term Catalogues on 28 May 1677, and published in quarto the same year. A second edition was entered on 26 November 1677. Some copies of this quarto have a title-page dated 1677 (Q2a), others a title-page dated 1678 and marked 'The second Edition' (Q2b); only signature C shows evidence of press correction.[1] The third quarto also exists in two states, one dated 1677 (Q3a), the other 1681 (Q3b). Both title-pages are marked 'The Third Edition' and both are 'Printed for *R. Bently* and *M. Magnes*'. As M. Magnes is not listed in the Term Catalogues before Easter 1679, the earlier date is clearly incorrect. Confirmation of the later date for this quarto comes from its advertisement page, which lists *The Policy of the Clergy of France to destroy the Protestants*, a book first entered in the Term Catalogues for Easter 1681. Once again, there is little evidence of press correction.[2] A fourth quarto appeared in 1686, a fifth in 1691, a sixth in 1694, a seventh in 1700, and an eighth in 1709; all are correctly numbered on their title-pages except the last, which is called 'The Sixth Edition'. Three octavo editions of *The Plain Dealer* were also published during Wycherley's lifetime. The first two, one dated 1710 and the other undated, are in fact Dutch piracies, printed at The Hague for Thomas Johnson. The third, a London edition of 1712, was bound up in the collected edition of Wycherley's *Works* of 1713; the catchword at the foot of the Epilogue links this play to *The Country Wife*, which followed next, and the pagination is continuous throughout.

The text deteriorates rapidly in these early editions. Q2 was set

[1] I. 521–2 go to with him (Q2a); go with him to (Q2b)
II. 74 isnow so cammon (Q2a); now is so common (Q2b)
II. 76 think they are (Q2a); think they're (Q2b)
II. 83 rididiculous (Q2a); ridiculous (Q2b)
II. 95–6 when she has (Q2a); when she says she has (Q2b)
II. 117 what   d (Q2a); what did (Q2b)
V. ii, 321 Both Q2a and Q2b drop the initial letter from 'in', which Hughes reports present in some American copies.
[2] I. 560 Riv alWives (Q3a); Rival Wives (Q3b)
III. 213 So icitor (Q3a); Solicitor (Q3b)
III. 504 Gurrdianless (Q3a); Guardianless (Q3b)
III. 544 Fellow)who (Q3a); Fellow (who (Q3b)
III. 565 andwe (Q3a); and we (Q3b)
IV. i, 341 shalt b ean (Q3a); shalt be an (Q3b)

from Q1, Q3 from Q2, and so on till Q8, which was set from Q4 with some reference to Q5 (which may explain its appearance as 'The Sixth Edition'). The London octavo follows Q1 more faithfully than any of the later quartos, but so many errors are present it is unlikely Wycherley himself corrected the printing. I have therefore taken as my copy-text a Bodleian copy of Q1 (Mal. B 273 (7)), collated against another Bodleian copy (4⁰ C 85 (4) Art) which has 'sure' at V. ii, 64, 'coaching' at V. ii 76, and 'fumblingf rigid' at II. 876. No other evidence of press correction was found. In the present edition, all press errors are silently amended, act and scene divisions regularized, and spelling and punctuation modernized throughout. A few exclamations are also regularized; thus I print hem for hemh, ha for hah, O for Oh, ay for I, and fie for fy. '*Aside*' appears on the same line as the speech prefix only when the entire speech is so delivered. To clarify the action, I have moved some stage directions to a more suitable place on the page, and added a few more. All editorial matter is enclosed within square brackets. Mr and Mrs are expanded throughout the play to Master and Mistress, which reflect contemporary pronunciation. The glosses record all significant departures of the present edition from Q1, together with a few rejected readings from the later quartos; over four hundred other variants, most of them showing the deterioration of the text in successive printings, are passed over in silence. Readings from Q8 are taken from the British Library copy, all other readings are from copies in the Bodleian Library, Oxford.

ABBREVIATIONS

Textual

ed.	editor
Q1	First quarto of 1677 (Q1a uncorrected, Q1b corrected)
Q2	Second quarto of 1677 (two states, Q2a dated 1677, Q2b dated 1678)
Q3	Third quarto of 1681 (two states, Q3a dated 1677, Q3b dated 1681)
Q4	Fourth quarto of 1686
Q5	Fifth quarto of 1691
Q6	Sixth quarto of 1694 (Q6a uncorrected, Q6b corrected)
Q7	Seventh quarto of 1700
Q8	Eighth quarto of 1709, marked 'The Sixth Edition'
O	London octavo of 1712
s.d.	stage direction
s.p.	speech prefix

Explanatory

B.E.	B.E., *A New Dictionary of the Terms Ancient and Modern of the Canting Crew* (1699)
Blount	Thomas Blount, *A Law-Dictionary* (1670)
Chamberlayne	Edward Chamberlayne, *Angliæ Notitia: or the Present State of England*, 2 vols. (1676)
Dennis	*The Critical Works of John Dennis,* ed. Edward Niles Hooker, 2 vols. (Baltimore, 1939–43)
OED	*Oxford English Dictionary*
Pack	Richardson Pack, 'Some memoirs of Mr Wycherley's life', prefixed to Wycherley's *Posthumous Works*, ed. Lewis Theobald (1728)
Phillips	Edward Phillips, *The New World of English Words: or, a General Dictionary* (1658)

FURTHER READING

Biography

Charles Perromat, *William Wycherley, Sa Vie—Son Oeuvre* (Paris, 1921).

Katharine M. Rogers, *William Wycherley* (New York, 1972).

Stage

Allardyce Nicoll, *A History of English Drama, 1660–1900*, I *1660–1700* (Cambridge, 1923), later revised.

The London Stage, 1660–1800, ed. W. Van Lennep, E. L. Avery, A. H. Scouten, G. Winchester Stone Jnr, and C. B. Hogan (Carbondale, Illinois, 1960–68).

Emmett L. Avery, '*The Plain Dealer* in the eighteenth century', *Research Studies of the State College of Washington*, XI (1943), 234–56.

Criticism

William Hazlitt, *Lectures on the English Comic Writers* (1819).

Bonamy Dobrée, *Restoration Comedy, 1660–1720* (Oxford, 1924).

Alexander H. Chorney, 'Wycherley's Manly reinterpreted', *Essays Critical and Historical Dedicated to Lily B. Campbell* (Berkeley and Los Angeles, 1950), pp. 161–9.

Norman N. Holland, *The First Modern Comedies* (1959).

Katharine M. Rogers, 'Fatal inconsistency: Wycherley and *The Plain-Dealer*', *A Journal of English Literary History*, XXVIII (1961), 148–62.

Rose A. Zimbardo, *Wycherley's Drama: a Link in the Development of English Satire* (1965).

Anne Righter, 'William Wycherley', *Restoration Theatre*, ed. John Russell Brown and Bernard Harris, Stratford-upon-Avon Studies, 6 (1965), pp. 71–91.

A. M. Friedson, 'Wycherley and Molière: satirical point of view in *The Plain Dealer*', *Modern Philology*, LXIV (1967), 189–97.

Virginia Ogden Birdsall, *Wild Civility: the English Comic Spirit on the Restoration Stage* (1970).

Ian Donaldson, *The World Upside-Down: Comedy from Jonson to Fielding* (Oxford, 1970), pp. 99–118.

John Loftis, Richard Southern, Marion Jones, and A. H. Scouten, *The Revels History of Drama in English, V: 1660–1750* (1976).
Peter Holland, *The Ornament of Action: text and performance in Restoration Comedy* (Cambridge, 1979).

No place of publication is given for books published solely or jointly in London.

THE
PLAIN-DEALER.

A
COMEDY.

As it is Acted at the
Theatre Royal.

Written by Mr WYCHERLEY.

HORAT.

—— *Ridiculum acre*
Fortius & melius magnas plerumque secat res.

Licensed *Jan.* 9. 1676.
ROGER L'ESTRANGE.

LONDON,

Printed by *T.N.* for *James Magnes* and *Rich. Bentley*
in *Russel-Street* in *Covent-garden* near the *Piazza's.*
M.DC.LXXVII.

ridiculum acri
fortius et melius magnas plerumque secat res.

---

acri Q2–8, O (acre Q1)

Motto

Jesting often cuts hard knots more forcefully and effectively than gravity (Horace, *Sat*. I. x. 14–15).

[THE EPISTLE DEDICATORY]

To my Lady B—

Madam,

Though I never had the honour to receive a favour from you, nay, or be known to you, I take the confidence of an author to write to you a *billet-doux* dedicatory, which is no new thing, 5 for by most dedications it appears that authors, though they praise their patrons from top to toe and seem to turn 'em inside out, know 'em as little as sometimes their patrons their books, though they read 'em out; and if the poetical daubers did not write the name of the man or woman on top of the 10 picture, 'twere impossible to guess whose it were. But you, madam, without the help of a poet, have made yourself known and famous in the world, and because you do not want it are therefore most worthy of an epistle dedicatory. And this play claims naturally your protection, since it has lost its reputation 15 with the ladies of stricter lives in the playhouse; and, you know, when men's endeavours are discountenanced and refused by the nice coy women of honour, they come to you; to you, the great and noble patroness of rejected and bashful men, of which number I profess myself to be one, though a 20 poet, a dedicating poet; to you, I say, madam, who have as discerning a judgment in what's obscene or not as any quick-sighted civil person of 'em all, and can make as much of a double-meaning saying as the best of 'em; yet would not, as some do, make nonsense of a poet's jest rather than not make 25 it bawdy, by which they show they as little value wit in a play as in a lover, provided they can bring t'other thing about. Their sense, indeed, lies all one way, and therefore are only for that in a poet which is moving, as they say. But what do they mean by that word 'moving'? Well, I must not put 'em to 30 the blush, since I find I can do't. In short, madam, you would not be one of those who ravish a poet's innocent words, and

----

1 *Lady B—* Mother Bennett, a celebrated procuress; Pepys describes
  her at work on 22 September 1660
21 *poet* author (frequent in Wycherley)
29 *moving* The innuendo is clarified in Farquhar's *The Beaux' Stratagem*
  (1707); when Dorinda boasts her lover 'spoke the softest moving
  things', Mrs Sullen replies 'Mine had his moving things too' (IV. i).

3

make 'em guilty of their own naughtiness, as 'tis termed, in
spite of his teeth. Nay, nothing is secure from the power of
their imaginations, no, not their husbands, whom they cuckold   35
with themselves by thinking of other men and so make the
lawful matrimonial embraces adultery, wrong husbands and
poets in thought and word, to keep their own reputations.
But your ladyship's justice, I know, would think a woman's
arraigning and damning a poet for her own obscenity like   40
her crying out a rape, and hanging a man for giving her
pleasure, only that she might be thought not to consent to't;
and so to vindicate her honour forfeits her modesty. But you,
madam, have too much modesty to pretend to't, though you
have as much to say for your modesty as many a nicer she,   45
for you never were seen at this play, no, not the first day;
and 'tis no matter what people's lives have been, they are un-
questionably modest who frequent not this play. For as
Master Bayes says of his, that it is the only touchstone of
men's wit and understanding, mine is, it seems, the only   50
touchstone of women's virtue and modesty. But hold, that
'touchstone' is equivocal, and by the strength of a lady's
imagination may become something that is not civil; but
your ladyship, I know, scorns to misapply a touchstone.
And, madam, though you have not seen this play, I hope   55
like other nice ladies you will the rather read it. Yet, lest the
chambermaid or page should not be trusted, and their indul-
gence could gain no further admittance for it than to their
ladies' lobbies or outward rooms, take it into your care and
protection, for by your recommendation and procurement it   60
may have the honour to get into their closets; for what they
renounce in public often entertains 'em there, with your help

---

33 *naughtiness* wickedness, depravity
41 *hanging a man* Rape was a felony punished by death.
45 *nicer she* more fastidious woman
49 *Bayes* the conceited dramatist in Buckingham's *The Rehearsal* (1671);
   he flatters Johnson with 'I know you have wit by the judgement you
   make of this Play; for that's the measure I go by: my Play is my
   Touch-stone' (III. i)
52 *touchstone* perhaps used in a *double entendre* for testicles
56–63 *Yet . . . especially* perhaps borrowed from Montaigne, *Essais*, III.
   v. (ed. M. Rat, 3 vols., Paris, 1952, III, 66): 'Je m'ennuie que mes
   Essais servent les dames de meuble commun seulement, et de meuble
   de sale. Ce chapitre me fera du cabinet'. G. B. Ives translates: 'It
   annoys me that the ladies use my Essays merely as a common piece
   of furniture, furniture for the reception-room. This chapter will make
   me suitable for the boudoir' (2 vols., New York, 1946, II, 1148)

especially. In fine, madam, for these and many other reasons, you are the fittest patroness or judge of this play, for you show no partiality to this or that author. For from some many 65 ladies will take a broad jest as cheerfully as from the watermen, and sit at some downright filthy plays, as they call 'em, as well satisfied and as still as a poet could wish 'em elsewhere. Therefore it must be the doubtful obscenity of my plays alone they take exceptions at, because it is too bashful for 'em; and 70 indeed most women hate men for attempting to halves on their chastity, and bawdy I find, like satire, should be home, not to have it taken notice of. But, now I mention satire, some there are who say 'tis the plain dealing of the play, not the obscenity, 'tis taking off the ladies' masks, not offering at their 75 petticoats, which offends 'em. And generally they are not the handsomest, or most innocent, who are the most angry at being discovered:

> *Nihil est audacius illis*
> *Deprensis: iram atque animos a crimine sumunt.* 80

Pardon, madam, the quotation, for a dedication can no more be without ends of Latin than flattery; and 'tis no matter whom it is writ to, for an author can as easily, I hope, suppose people to have more understanding and languages than they have, as well as more virtues. But why the devil should 85 any of the few modest and handsome be alarmed? (For some there are who as well as any deserve those attributes, yet refrain not from seeing this play, nor think it any addition to their virtue to set up for it in a playhouse, lest there it should look too much like acting.) But why, I say, should any at all of 90 the truly virtuous be concerned, if those who are not so are distinguished from 'em? For by that mask of modesty which women wear promiscuously in public, they are all alike, and you can no more know a kept wench from a woman of

---

80 Deprensis ed. (*Deprehensis* Q1–8, 0)
89 *lest there* Q1, 0 (lest Q2–8)

---

63 *In fine* in short, to sum up (frequent in Wycherley)
66–7 *watermen* The Thames boatmen habitually attacked other fares with obscene abuse; the joke was to reply in kind.
71 *to halves* by halves, imperfectly
72 *home* searching, trenchant
79–80 *Nihil . . . sumunt* There's no effrontery like that of a woman caught in the act; her very guilt inspires her with wrath and insolence (Juvenal, *Sat.* vi. 284–5).
89 *set up for* support
93 *promiscuously* indiscriminately

honour by her looks than by her dress. For those who are   95
of quality without honour, if any such there are, they have
their quality to set off their false modesty as well as their false
jewels, and you must no more suspect their countenances for
counterfeit than their pendants, though, as the plain dealer
Montaigne says,   100

> *Elles envoyent leur conscience au bordel, et tiennent
> leur contenance en règle.*

But those who act as they look ought not to be scandalized
at the reprehension of others' faults, lest they tax themselves
with 'em, and by too delicate and quick an apprehension not   105
only make that obscene which I meant innocent, but that
satire on all which was intended only on those who deserved
it. But, madam, I beg your pardon for this digression to civil
women and ladies of honour, since you and I shall never be
the better for 'em; for a comic poet and a lady of your pro-   110
fession make most of the other sort, and the stage and your
houses, like our plantations, are propagated by the least nice
women; and, as with the ministers of justice, the vices of the
age are our best business. But now I mention public persons,
I can no longer defer doing you the justice of a dedication   115
and telling you your own, who are, of all public-spirited
people, the most necessary, most communicative, most
generous and hospitable. Your house has been the house of
the people, your sleep still disturbed for the public, and when
you arose 'twas that others might lie down, and you waked   120
that others might rest. The good you have done is unspeakable. How many young, unexperienced heirs have you
kept from rash, foolish marriages, and from being jilted for
their lives by the worst sort of jilts, wives? How many unbe-
witched widowers' children have you preserved from the   125
tyranny of stepmothers? How many old dotards from

---

101 Elles envoyent Q2 (*Els envoy* Q1, 0; *Eles envoyent* Q3–8)

101–2 *Elles . . . règle Essais,* III. v. (ed. cit., III, 65); Wycherley rewrites
Montaigne, making women, not men, the subject; G. B. Ives translates: 'Men send their conscience to the brothel and keep their
demeanour in good order' (ed. cit., II, 1147)
112 *plantations* Statutes entitled some female felons to choose between
transportation and execution.
116 *your own* the plain truth about yourself (usually in a bad sense)
117 *communicative* (1) informative (2) sharing, i.e., fornicating (and perhaps passing on venereal disease)
119 *still* continually
120 *waked* stayed awake, kept watch

cuckoldage, and keeping other men's wenches and children?
How many adulteries and unnatural sins have you prevented?
In fine, you have been a constant scourge to the old lecher,
and often a terror to the young; you have made concupiscence 130
its own punishment, and extinguished lust with lust, like
blowing up of houses to stop the fire.

*Nimirum, propter continentiam incontinentia necessaria
est, incendium ignibus extinguetur.*

There's Latin for you again, madam. I protest to you, as I 135
am an author, I cannot help it. Nay, I can hardly keep myself
from quoting Aristotle and Horace, and talking to you of the
rules of writing (like the French authors), to show you and
my reader I understand 'em in my epistle, lest neither of you
should find it out by the play; and according to the rules of 140
dedications, 'tis no matter whether you understand or no what
I quote or say to you of writing, for an author can as easily
make anyone a judge or critic in an epistle as an hero in his
play. But, madam, that this may prove to the end a true
epistle dedicatory, I'd have you know 'tis not without a design 145
upon you which is in the behalf of the fraternity of
Parnassus: that songs and sonnets may go at your houses and
in your liberties for guineas and half-guineas, and that wit,
at least with you, as of old, may be the price of beauty; and
so you will prove a true encourager of poetry, for love is a 150
better help to it than wine, and poets, like painters, draw
better after the life than by fancy. Nay, in justice, madam,

134 extinguetur ed. (*extinguitur* Q1–8, 0)
139 *reader* Q2–8, 0 (readers Q1)

132 *blowing . . . fire* During the Fire of 2–6 September 1666, houses at
   risk were pulled down with hooks and blown up with gunpowder to
   make a gap the flames could not leap.
133–4 *Nimirum . . . extinguetur* No doubt it is for the sake of continence
   that incontinence is necessary; no doubt a fire will be extinguished
   by flames.—Tertullian, *De Pudicitia,* I. xvi. (ed. J.-P. Migne, Paris,
   1878, col. 1034; tr. W. P. le Saint, London, 1959, p. 56); Wycherley
   probably read it in Montaigne, *Essais*, III. v. (ed. cit., III, 79), which
   also prints *extinguitur* for *extinguetur*; Q1 sets out the Tertullian as
   verse.
138 *French authors* The 1660 edition of Pierre Corneille's *Théâtre* included three *Discours sur le poème dramatique* and *Examens* to
   individual plays; many of Jean Racine's masterpieces between *Andro-
   maque* (1667) and *Phèdre* (1677) were published with critical pre-
   faces.
148 *liberties* districts outside the city, where most London brothels were
   situated

I think a poet ought to be as free of your houses as of the
playhouses, since he contributes to the support of both and is
as necessary to such as you as a ballad-singer to a pickpurse,   155
in convening the cullies at the theatres, to be picked up and
carried to supper and bed at your houses. And, madam, the
reason of this motion of mine is because poor poets can get
no favour in the tiring-rooms, for they are no keepers, you
know; and folly and money, the old enemies of wit, are   160
even too hard for it on its own dunghill; and for other ladies,
a poet can least go to the price of them. Besides, his wit,
which ought to recommend him to 'em, is as much an obstruc-
tion to his love as to his wealth or preferment, for most
women nowadays apprehend wit in a lover as much as in a   165
husband. They hate a man that knows 'em. They must have a
blind, easy fool whom they can lead by the nose, and, as the
Scythian women of old, must baffle a man and put out his
eyes ere they will lie with him; and then too, like thieves,
when they have plundered and stripped a man, leave him.   170
But if there should be one of an hundred of those ladies
generous enough to give herself to a man that has more wit
than money, all things considered, he would think it cheaper
coming to you for a mistress, though you made him pay his
guinea; as a man in a journey, out of good husbandry, had   175
better pay for what he has in an inn than lie on free cost at a
gentleman's house.

In fine, madam, like a faithful dedicator I hope I have done
myself right in the first place, then you and your profession,

---

155 *a pickpurse* Q8, 0 (the pickpurse Q1–7)

153–4 *free . . . playhouses* Dramatists were often admitted to the
theatres free.
155 *ballad-singer . . . pickpurse* One draws and diverts the crowd while
the other robs them.
156 *cullies* gulls dupes (frequent in Wycherley)
159 *tiring-rooms* dressing-rooms
159 *keepers* men who keep mistresses
167 *nose* perhaps used in a *double entendre* for penis
168 *Scythian women* Wycherley here borrows again from Montaigne,
Essais, III. v. (ed. cit., III, 88), which G. B. Ives translates: 'The
Scythian women put out the eyes of all their slaves and prisoners of
war, to make use of them more freely and more secretly' (ed. cit., II,
1174).
168 *baffle* hoodwink
168–9 *put out his eyes* used with a sidelong reference to blindness caused
by venereal disease
176 *on free cost* cost-free; tipping the servants would cost a guest more
than his bill at an inn

which in the wisest and most religious government of the   180
world is honoured with the public allowance, and in those
that are thought the most uncivilized and barbarous is pro-
tected and supported by the ministers of justice. And of you,
madam, I ought to say no more here, for your virtues deserve
a poem rather than an epistle, or a volume entire to give the   185
world your memoirs or life at large, and which (upon the word
of an author that has a mind to make an end of his dedication) I promise to do when I write the annals of our British
love, which shall be dedicated to the ladies concerned if they
will not think them something too obscene too, when your   190
life, compared with many that are thought innocent, I doubt
not may vindicate you and me to the world for the confidence
I have taken in this address to you, which then may be
thought neither impertinent nor immodest. And, whatsoever
your amorous misfortunes have been, none can charge you   195
with that heinous and worst of women's crimes, hypocrisy;
nay, in spite of misfortunes or age, you are the same woman
still, though most of your sex grow Magdalens at fifty and, as
a solid French author has it,

> *Après le plaisir vient la peine,*   200
> *Après la peine, la vertu.*

But sure, an old sinner's continency is much like a gamester's
forswearing play when he has lost all his money, and modesty
is a kind of a youthful dress which, as it makes a young
woman more amiable, makes an old one more nauseous; a   205
bashful old woman is like an hopeful old man, and the
affected chastity of antiquated beauties is rather a reproach
than an honour to 'em, for it shows the men's virtue only,
not theirs. But you, in fine, madam, are no more an hypocrite
than I am when I praise you; therefore I doubt not will be   210
thought even by yours and the play's enemies, the nicest
ladies, to be the fittest patroness for,

madam,

your ladyship's most obedient,

faithful, humble servant, and   215

THE PLAIN DEALER.

198 *Magdalens* reformed prostitutes, named after Mary of Magdala
    (Luke, viii. 2; usually identified with the 'sinner' of Luke, vii. 37–8)
199 *French author* unidentified
200–1 *Après . . . vertu* After pleasure comes pain, after pain virtue.

THE PERSONS

MANLY, *of an honest, surly, nice humour, supposed first, in the time of the Dutch war, to have procured the command of a ship out of honour, not interest, and choosing a sea life only to avoid the world*	Mr Hart

5

FREEMAN, *Manly's lieutenant, a gentle-man well educated, but of a broken fortune, a complier with the age*   Mr Kynaston

VERNISH, *Manly's bosom and only friend*   Mr Griffin   10

NOVEL, *a pert, railing coxcomb and an admirer of novelties; makes love to Olivia*   Mr Clark

MAJOR OLDFOX, *an old, impertinent fop, given to scribbling; makes love to the Widow Blackacre*   Mr Cartwright   15

MY LORD PLAUSIBLE, *a ceremonious, supple, commending coxcomb, in love with Olivia*   Mr Haines

JERRY BLACKACRE, *a true raw squire, under age and his mother's govern-ment, bred to the law*   Mr Charlton   20

[SERJEANT PLODDON
[QUAINT
[BLUNDER
[PETULANT   *lawyers*]   25
[BUTTONGOWN
[SPLITCAUSE

---

1 *nice humour* strict temperament

2–3 *Dutch war* probably the third Anglo-Dutch war of 1672–74; Captain Wycherley served in the second campaign

10 VERNISH i.e., varnish, 'a specious gloss or outward show; a pretence' (*OED*)

14 OLDFOX 'a subtil old Fellow; also an old broad Sword' (*B.E.*)

17 PLAUSIBLE 'smooth, specious, Taking' (*B.E.*)

23 PLODDON cf. *'Plodder,* a Porer in Records, Writings or Books, a dull Drudge' (*B.E.*)

28 SPLITCAUSE cf. *'Splitter-of-Causes,* a Lawyer' (*B.E.*)

11

OLIVIA, *Manly's mistress*	*Mrs Marshall*	
FIDELIA, *in love with Manly, and followed*	*Mrs Boutell*	30
him to sea in man's clothes		
ELIZA, *cousin to Olivia*	*Mrs Knepp*	
LETTICE, *Olivia's woman*	*Mrs Knight*	
THE WIDOW BLACKACRE, *a petulant liti-*	*Mrs Corey*	
gious widow, always in law, and mother		35
to Squire Jerry		

LAWYERS, KNIGHTS OF THE POST, BAILIFFS, AN ALDERMAN,
A BOOKSELLER'S PRENTICE, A FOOTBOY [*to Olivia*], SAILORS,
WAITERS, [A CONSTABLE] *and* ATTENDANTS

The scene: London   40

---

30 FIDELIA sincerity, trust, faithfulness (from Latin *fidelis*)
34 BLACKACRE arbitrary name for a parcel of land, used in stating hypo-
thetical law cases
37 KNIGHTS OF THE POST professional false witnesses, 'Irish Evidence'
(*B.E.*); they admit perjury, forgery, and fraud in V. ii. 389–92.

PROLOGUE

Spoken by the Plain Dealer

I the Plain Dealer am to act today,
And my rough part begins before the play.
First, you who scribble, yet hate all that write,
And keep each other company in spite,
As rivals in your common mistress, fame,   5
And with faint praises one another damn;
'Tis a good play, we know, you can't forgive,
But grudge yourselves the pleasure you receive:
Our scribbler therefore bluntly bid me say
He would not have the wits pleased here today.   10
Next you, the fine, loud gentlemen o'th' pit
Who damn all plays, yet if y'ave any wit
'Tis but what here you sponge, and daily get;
Poets, like friends to whom you are in debt,
You hate; and so rooks laugh, to see undone   15
Those pushing gamesters whom they live upon.
Well, you are sparks, and still will be i'th' fashion:
Rail then at plays, to hide your obligation.
Now, you shrewd judges who the boxes sway,   ⎫
Leading the ladies' hearts and sense astray,   ⎬   20
And, for their sakes, see all, and hear no play: ⎭
Correct your cravats, foretops, lock behind,
The dress and breeding of the play ne'er mind;
Plain dealing is, you'll say, quite out of fashion;
You'll hate it here, as in a dedication.   25
And your fair neighbours in a limning poet
No more than in a painter will allow it.
Pictures too like, the ladies will not please,
They must be drawn too here like goddesses;

Prologue addressing the critics (3) and fops (11) in the pit, then Society
    escorts (19) in the boxes; the citizens and footmen in the galleries
    are ignored
13 *sponge* steal (from the dramatists)
15 *rooks* sharpers, swindlers (frequent in Wycherley)
22 *foretops* real or false locks decorating the forehead
26 *limning poet* author of character sketches

You, as at Lely's too, would truncheon wield,   30
And look like heroes in a painted field.
But the coarse dauber of the coming scenes
To follow life and nature only means;
Displays you as you are: makes his fine woman
A mercenary jilt, and true to no man;   35
His men of wit and pleasure of the age
Are as dull rogues as ever cumbered stage;
He draws a friend only to custom just,
And makes him naturally break his trust.
I, only, act a part like none of you,   40
And yet, you'll say, it is a fool's part too:
An honest man who like you never winks
At faults, but unlike you speaks what he thinks;
The only fool who ne'er found patron yet,
For truth is now a fault as well as wit.   45
And where else but on stages do we see
Truth pleasing, or rewarded honesty?
Which our bold poet does this day in me.
If not to th' honest, be to th' prosp'rous kind:
Some friends at court let the Plain Dealer find.   50

---

30 *Lely* Peter Lely (1618–80), the fashionable portrait-painter of celebrated beauties like the Duchess of Cleveland (at Hampton Court)
  and heroic generals like Sir George Ayscue, complete with truncheon
  (at Greenwich); an engraving of his portrait of Wycherley is reproduced as the Frontispiece
30 *truncheon* baton carried as symbol of military command
38 *just* faithful, true

THE PLAIN DEALER

Act I, Scene i

CAPTAIN MANLY'S *Lodging*
Enter CAPTAIN MANLY, *surlily, and my* LORD PLAUSIBLE
following him, and two SAILORS *behind*

MANLY

Tell not me, my good Lord Plausible, of your decorums,
supercilious forms, and slavish ceremonies; your little tricks
which you, the spaniels of the world, do daily over and over
for and to one another, not out of love or duty, but your
servile fear.   5

LORD PLAUSIBLE

Nay, i'faith, i'faith, you are too passionate, and I must
humbly beg your pardon and leave to tell you they are the
arts and rules the prudent of the world walk by.

MANLY

Let 'em. But I'll have no leading-strings; I can walk alone.
I hate a harness, and will not tag on in a faction, kissing my   10
leader behind, that another slave may do the like to me.

LORD PLAUSIBLE

What, will you be singular then, like nobody? follow, love,
and esteem nobody?

MANLY

Rather than be general, like you: follow everybody, court
and kiss everybody, though perhaps at the same time you   15
hate everybody.

LORD PLAUSIBLE

Why, seriously, with your pardon, my dear friend—

MANLY

With your pardon, my no friend, I will not, as you do,
whisper my hatred or my scorn, call a man fool or knave by
signs or mouths over his shoulder, whilst you have him in   20
your arms; for such as you, like common whores and pickpockets, are only dangerous to those you embrace.

10 *tag* ed. (tug Q1–8, 0)
12 *follow, love* ed. (follow Love Q1–8, 0)

9 *leading-strings* reins to guide children learning to walk

LORD PLAUSIBLE

Such as I? Heavens defend me! Upon my honour—

MANLY

Upon your title, my lord, if you'd have me believe you.

LORD PLAUSIBLE

Well then, as I am a person of honour, I never attempted to   25
abuse or lessen any person in my life.

MANLY

What, you were afraid?

LORD PLAUSIBLE

No, but seriously, I hate to do a rude thing; no, faith, I speak
well of all mankind.

MANLY

I thought so; but know, that speaking well of all mankind is   30
the worst kind of detraction, for it takes away the reputation
of the few good men in the world by making all alike. Now
I speak ill of most men because they deserve it, I that can
do a rude thing rather than an unjust thing.

LORD PLAUSIBLE

Well, tell not me, my dear friend, what people deserve; I   35
ne'er mind that. I, like an author in a dedication, never speak
well of a man for his sake, but my own; I will not disparage
any man to disparage myself, for to speak ill of people
behind their backs is not like a person of honour, and, truly,
to speak ill of 'em to their faces is not like a complaisant   40
person. But if I did say or do an ill thing to anybody, it
should be sure to be behind their backs, out of pure good
manners.

MANLY

Very well; but I, that am an unmannerly sea-fellow, if I ever
speak well of people, which is very seldom indeed, it should   45
be sure to be behind their backs; and if I would say or do ill
to any, it should be to their faces. I would justle a proud,
strutting, over-looking coxcomb at the head of his sycophants, rather than put out my tongue at him when he were
past me; would frown in the arrogant, big, dull face of an   50
overgrown knave of business, rather than vent my spleen
against him when his back were turned; would give fawning
slaves the lie whilst they embrace or commend me; cowards,
whilst they brag; call a rascal by no other title though his

48 *over-looking* disdainful
50-1 *an overgrown . . . business* a pompous, unscrupulous man of
    affairs

father had left him a duke's; laugh at fools aloud before their   55
mistresses; and must desire people to leave me, when their
visits grow at last as troublesome as they were at first
impertinent.

LORD PLAUSIBLE

I would not have my visits troublesome.

MANLY

The only way to be sure not to have 'em troublesome is to   60
make 'em when people are not at home, for your visits, like
other good turns, are most obliging when made or done to
a man in his absence. A pox! Why should anyone, because
he has nothing to do, go and disturb another man's business?

LORD PLAUSIBLE

I beg your pardon, my dear friend. What, you have business?   65

MANLY

If you have any, I would not detain your lordship.

LORD PLAUSIBLE

Detain me, dear sir! I can never have enough of your
company.

MANLY

I'm afraid I should be tiresome. I know not what you think.

LORD PLAUSIBLE

Well, dear sir, I see you would have me gone.   70

MANLY *(Aside)*

But I see you won't.

LORD PLAUSIBLE

Your most faithful—

MANLY

God be w'ye, my lord.

LORD PLAUSIBLE

Your most humble—

MANLY

Farewell.   75

LORD PLAUSIBLE

And eternally—

MANLY

And eternally ceremony. *(Aside)* Then the devil take thee
eternally.

LORD PLAUSIBLE

You shall use no ceremony, by my life.

MANLY

I do not intend it.   80

---

73 *God be w'ye* God be with you, not yet contracted to *Good-bye*

LORD PLAUSIBLE

Why do you stir, then?

MANLY

Only to see you out of doors, that I may shut 'em against more welcomes.

LORD PLAUSIBLE

Nay, faith, that shan't pass upon your most faithful, humble servant.   85

MANLY *(Aside)*

Nor this any more upon me.

LORD PLAUSIBLE

Well, you are too strong for me.

MANLY *(Aside)*

I'd sooner be visited by the plague, for that only would keep a man from visits and his doors shut.

(Exit, thrusting out my LORD PLAUSIBLE*)*

Manent SAILORS

1 SAILOR

Here's a finical fellow, Jack. What a brave fair-weather   90
captain of a ship he would make!

2 SAILOR

He, a captain of a ship! It must be when she's in the dock then, for he looks like one of those that get the king's commissions for hulls to sell a king's ship, when a brave fellow has fought her almost to a longboat.   95

1 SAILOR

On my conscience then, Jack, that's the reason our bully tar sunk our ship: not only that the Dutch might not have her, but that the courtiers, who laugh at wooden legs, might not make her prize.

2 SAILOR

A pox of his sinking, Tom; we have made a base, broken,   100
short voyage of it.

1 SAILOR

Ay, your brisk dealers in honour always make quick returns with their ship to the dock and their men to the hospitals.

---

84 *pass upon* impose upon, gain credit with
90 *finical* over-fastidious
93–4 *commissions for hulls* Charles II gave friends the rights to sell dismantled ships; Pepys received one while Secretary of the Navy Board.
95 *longboat* where a ship's crew under attack would make a last stand before escaping

'Tis, let me see, just a month since we set out of the river,
and the wind was almost as cross to us as the Dutch.   105

2 SAILOR

Well, I forgive him sinking my own poor truck, if he would
but have given me time and leave to have saved black Kate
of Wapping's small venture.

1 SAILOR

Faith, I forgive him, since, as the purser told me, he sunk
the value of five or six thousand pound of his own with   110
which he was to settle himself somewhere in the Indies; for
our merry lieutenant was to succeed him in his commission
for the ship back, for he was resolved never to return again
for England.

2 SAILOR

So it seemed, by his fighting.   115

1 SAILOR

No, but he was aweary of this side of the world here, they
say.

2 SAILOR

Ay, or else he would not have bid so fair for a passage into
t'other.

1 SAILOR

Jack, thou think'st thyself in the forecastle, thou'rt so wag- 120
gish. But I tell you then, he had a mind to go live and bask
himself on the sunny side of the globe.

2 SAILOR

What, out of any discontent? For he's always as dogged as
an old tarpaulin when hindered of a voyage by a young
pantaloon captain.   125

1 SAILOR

'Tis true, I never saw him pleased but in the fight; and then
he looked like one of us coming from the pay-table, with a

---

106 *truck* goods for trading
108 *Wapping* seamen's hamlet on the Thames below the Tower
111 *Indies* Manly's ship fell to the Dutch while acting as convoy to an
    East India merchantman probably bound for Java, Sumatra, or
    Bombay.
113 *back* i.e., on the home voyage
123 *dogged* ill-tempered, morose (frequent in Wycherley)
125 *pantaloon captain* Commissions given to unfledged 'gentlemen'
    captains (in fashionable pantaloon breeches) were resented by dis-
    placed 'tarpaulings of Wapping and Blackwall, from whence the
    good commanders of old were all used to be chosen' (Pepys, quoted
    in David Ogg, *England in the Reign of Charles II*, 2 vols. (Oxford,
    1956), I. p. 272)

new lining to our hats under our arms.

2 SAILOR

A pox! He's like the Bay of Biscay, rough and angry let the
wind blow where 'twill. 130

1 SAILOR

Nay, there's no more dealing with him than with the land in
a storm; no near!

2 SAILOR

'Tis a hurry-durry blade. Dost thou remember, after we had
tugged hard the old, leaky longboat to save his life, when I
welcomed him ashore, he gave me a box on the ear and 135
called me fawning water-dog?

Enter MANLY *and* FREEMAN

1 SAILOR

Hold thy peace, Jack, and stand by; the foul weather's
coming.

MANLY

You rascals! dogs! how could this tame thing get through
you? 140

1 SAILOR

Faith, to tell your honour the truth, we were at hob in the
hall, and whilst my brother and I were quarrelling about a
cast he slunk by us.

2 SAILOR

He's a sneaking fellow, I warrant for't.

MANLY

Have more care for the future, you slaves. Go, and with 145
drawn cutlasses stand at the stair-foot and keep all that ask
for me from coming up; suppose you were guarding the
scuttle to the powder-room; let none enter here, at your and
their peril.

1 SAILOR

No, for the danger would be the same: you would blow 150
them and us up if we should.

2 SAILOR

Must no one come to you, sir?

128 *lining to our hats* 'in steps another of the *Tarpauling Fraternity*,
with his Hat under his Arm, half full of Money' (Ned Ward, *The
London Spy*, ed. Ralph Straus (1924), p. 332)
132 *no near* 'a command to the helmsman to come no closer to the
wind' (*OED*); here=look out! Perhaps he hears Manly returning.
133 *hurry-durry blade* boisterous fellow
141 *hob* quoits, probably played here with coins for rings and an impro-
vised target or 'hob'

MANLY

No man, sir.

1 SAILOR

No man, sir; but a woman then, an't like your honour—

MANLY

No woman neither, you impertinent dog. Would you be 155
pimping? A sea-pimp is the strangest monster she has.

2 SAILOR

Indeed, an't like your honour, 'twill be hard for us to deny
a woman anything, since we are so newly come on shore.

1 SAILOR

We'll let no old woman come up, though it were our trusting
landlady at Wapping. 160

MANLY

Would you be witty, you brandy casks you? You become a
jest as ill as you do a horse. Begone, you dogs! I hear a noise
on the stairs. *(Exeunt* SAILORS*)*

FREEMAN

Faith, I am sorry you would let the fop go; I intended to
have had some sport with him. 165

MANLY

Sport with him! A pox, then why did you not stay? You
should have enjoyed your coxcomb and had him to yourself,
for me.

FREEMAN

No, I should not have cared for him without you neither,
for the pleasure which fops afford is like that of drinking, 170
only good when 'tis shared; and a fool, like a bottle, which
would make you merry in company, will make you dull
alone. But how the devil could you turn a man of his quality
down stairs? You use a lord with very little ceremony, it
seems. 175

MANLY

A lord! What, thou art one of those who esteem men only
by the marks and value fortune has set upon 'em, and never
consider intrinsic worth. But counterfeit honour will not be
current with me; I weigh the man, not his title; 'tis not the
king's stamp can make the metal better or heavier. Your lord 180
is a leaden shilling, which you may bend every way, and
debases the stamp he bears instead of being raised by't.—
Here again, you slaves?

Enter SAILORS

1 SAILOR

Only to receive farther instructions, an't like your honour.
What if a man should bring you money, should we turn him   185
back?

MANLY

All men, I say. Must I be pestered with you too? You dogs,
away.

2 SAILOR

Nay, I know one man your honour would not have us hinder
coming to you, I'm sure.   190

MANLY

Who's that? Speak quickly, slaves.

2 SAILOR

Why, a man that should bring you a challenge, for though
you refuse money, I'm sure you love fighting too well to
refuse that.

MANLY

Rogue! rascal! dog!   *(Kicks the* SAILORS *out)*   195

FREEMAN

Nay, let the poor rogues have their forecastle jests; they
cannot help 'em in a fight, scarce when a ship's sinking.

MANLY

Damn their untimely jests. A servant's jest is more sauciness
than his counsel.

FREEMAN

But what, will you see nobody? Not your friends?   200

MANLY

Friends? I have but one, and he, I hear, is not in town; nay,
can have but one friend, for a true heart admits but of one
friendship as of one love. But in having that friend I have a
thousand, for he has the courage of men in despair, yet the
diffidency and caution of cowards, the secrecy of the revenge-   205
ful and the constancy of martyrs: one fit to advise, to keep
a secret, to fight and die for his friend. Such I think him, for
I have trusted him with my mistress in my absence, and the
trust of beauty is sure the greatest we can show.

FREEMAN

Well, but all your good thoughts are not for him alone, I   210
hope. Pray, what d'ye think of me for a friend?

MANLY

Of thee! Why, thou art a latitudinarian in friendship, that is,

212 *latitudinarian* a liberal churchman 'that is no Slave to Rubrick,
Canons, Liturgy, or Oath of Canonical Obedience' (*B.E.*); Manly
suggests Freeman has so many friends the term is meaningless

no friend; thou dost side with all mankind, but wilt suffer for
none. Thou art indeed like your Lord Plausible, the pink of
courtesy, therefore hast no friendship; for ceremony and   215
great professing renders friendship as much suspected as it
does religion.

FREEMAN

And no professing, no ceremony at all in friendship were as
unnatural and as undecent as in religion; and there is hardly
such a thing as an honest hypocrite, who professes himself   220
to be worse than he is, unless it be yourself; for though I
could never get you to say you were my friend, I know
you'll prove so.

MANLY

I must confess I am so much your friend I would not deceive
you; therefore must tell you, not only because my heart is   225
taken up but according to your rules of friendship, I cannot
be your friend.

FREEMAN

Why, pray?

MANLY

Because he that is, you'll say, a true friend to a man is a
friend to all his friends. But you must pardon me; I cannot   230
wish well to pimps, flatterers, detractors, and cowards, stiff,
nodding knaves and supple, pliant, kissing fools. Now, all
these I have seen you use like the dearest friends in the world.

FREEMAN

Ha ha ha! What, you observed me, I warrant, in the galleries at Whitehall, doing the business of the place? Pshaw!   235
Court professions, like court promises, go for nothing, man.
But, faith, could you think I was a friend to all those I
hugged, kissed, flattered, bowed to? Ha ha—

MANLY

You told 'em so, and swore it too; I heard you.

FREEMAN

Ay, but when their backs were turned did I not tell you they   240
were rogues, villains, rascals, whom I despised and hated?

216 *professing* avowal, declaration
226 *taken up* i.e., by Vernish, 'for a true heart admits but of one friend-
     ship' (202–3)
235 *Whitehall* The picture galleries of the royal palace at Whitehall
     were the setting for its largest social gatherings; on 6 February
     1685 Evelyn records 'unexpressable luxury, & prophaneße, gaming,
     & all dissolution' there.

MANLY

Very fine! But what reason had I to believe you spoke your
heart to me, since you professed deceiving so many?

FREEMAN

Why, don't you know, good captain, that telling truth is a
quality as prejudicial to a man that would thrive in the world   245
as square play to a cheat or true love to a whore? Would
you have a man speak truth to his ruin? You are severer
than the law, which requires no man to swear against himself. You would have me speak truth against myself, I
warrant, and tell my promising friend, the courtier, he has   250
a bad memory?

MANLY

Yes.

FREEMAN

And so make him remember to forget my business. And I
should tell the great lawyer too that he takes oftener fees to
hold his tongue, than to speak?   255

MANLY

No doubt on't.

FREEMAN

Ay, and have him hang or ruin me, when he should come to
be a judge and I before him. And you would have me tell
the new officer, who bought his employment lately, that he
is a coward?   260

MANLY

Ay.

FREEMAN

And so get myself cashiered, not him, he having the better
friends though I the better sword. And I should tell the
scribbler of honour that heraldry were a prettier and fitter
study for so fine a gentleman than poetry?   265

MANLY

Certainly.

FREEMAN

And so find myself mauled in his next hired lampoon. And
you would have me tell the holy lady too she lies with her
chaplain?

MANLY

No doubt on't.   270

246 *square* honest
264 *scribbler of honour* titled author

FREEMAN

And so draw the clergy upon my back, and want a good
table to dine at sometimes. And by the same reason too I
should tell you that the world thinks you a madman, a
brutal, and have you cut my throat, or worse, hate me. What
other good success of all my plain dealing could I have, than   275
what I've mentioned?

MANLY

Why, first, your promising courtier would keep his word out
of fear of more reproaches, or at least would give you no
more vain hopes; your lawyer would serve you more faithfully, for he, having no honour but his interest, is truest still   280
to him he knows suspects him; the new officer would provoke
thee to make him a coward and so be cashiered, that thou,
or some other honest fellow who had more courage than
money, might get his place; the noble sonneteer would
trouble thee no more with his madrigals; the praying lady   285
would leave off railing at wenching before thee, and not turn
away her chamber-maid for her own known frailty with thee;
and I, instead of hating thee, should love thee for thy plain
dealing; and in lieu of being mortified am proud that the
world and I think not well of one another.   290

FREEMAN

Well, doctors differ. You are for plain dealing, I find; but
against your particular notions I have the practice of the
whole world. Observe but any morning what people do when
they get together on the Exchange, in Westminster Hall, or
the galleries in Whitehall.   295

MANLY

I must confess, there they seem to rehearse Bayes's grand
dance: here you see a bishop bowing low to a gaudy atheist;

274 *brutal* a noun = a brutal person
275 *good success* prosperous result
286–7 *turn away* dismiss
294–5 *Exchange . . . Whitehall* rendezvous for merchants at the Royal
   Exchange in Cornhill (or fashionable shoppers if the New Exchange in the Strand is meant), lawyers at Westminster Hall, and
   courtiers at Whitehall
296 *rehearse* repeat, with a punning reference to Buckingham's play
296–7 *Bayes's grand dance* In Buckingham's *The Rehearsal* (1671), two
   Kings of Brentford descend from the clouds and '*Dance a grand
   Dance*'; the dramatist Bayes comments: 'This, now, is an ancient
   Dance . . . deriv'd, with a little alteration, to the Inns of Court'
   (V.i).
297 *gaudy* showy, flashy

a judge to a door-keeper; a great lord to a fishmonger, or a scrivener with a jack-chain about his neck; a lawyer to a serjeant at arms; a velvet physician to a threadbare chemist; 300 and a supple gentleman-usher to a surly beef-eater; and so tread round in a preposterous huddle of ceremony to each other, whilst they can hardly hold their solemn false countenances.

FREEMAN

Well, they understand the world. 305

MANLY

Which I do not, I confess.

FREEMAN

But sir, pray believe the friendship I promise you real, whatsoever I have professed to others. Try me, at least.

MANLY

Why, what would you do for me?

FREEMAN

I would fight for you. 310

MANLY

That you would do for your own honour. But what else?

FREEMAN

I would lend you money, if I had it.

MANLY

To borrow more of me another time. That were but putting your money to interest; a usurer would be as good a friend. But what other piece of friendship? 315

FREEMAN

I would speak well of you to your enemies.

MANLY

To encourage others to be your friends by a show of gratitude. But what else?

FREEMAN

Nay, I would not hear you ill spoken of behind your back by my friend. 320

MANLY

Nay, then thou'rt a friend indeed; but it were unreasonable

---

299 *jack-chain* decorative chain with each link a double loop of un-welded wire
300 *serjeant at arms* Parliamentary officer empowered to arrest offenders, etc.
300 *chemist* alchemist
301 *gentleman-usher* gentleman attending upon someone of superior rank
301 *beef-eater* 'a well-fed menial' (*OED*)

to expect it from thee as the world goes now, when new
friends, like new mistresses, are got by disparaging old ones.

Enter FIDELIA [*in man's clothes*]

But here comes another will say as much at least.—Dost
not thou love me devilishly too, my little volunteer, as well   325
as he or any man can?

FIDELIA

Better than any man can love you, my dear captain.

MANLY [*To* FREEMAN]

Look you there, I told you so.

FIDELIA

As well as you do truth or honour, sir; as well.

MANLY

Nay, good young gentleman, enough, for shame! Thou hast   330
been a page, by thy flattering and lying, to one of those
praying ladies who love flattery so well they are jealous of it,
and wert turned away for saying the same things to the old
housekeeper for sweetmeats as you did to your lady; for thou
flatterest everything and everybody alike.   335

FIDELIA

You, dear sir, should not suspect the truth of what I say of
you, though to you. Fame, the old liar, is believed when she
speaks wonders of you; you cannot be flattered, sir; your
merit is unspeakable.

MANLY

Hold, hold, sir, or I shall suspect worse of you: that you   340
have been a cushion-bearer to some state hypocrite, and
turned away by the chaplains for out-flattering their probation sermons for a benefice.

FIDELIA

Suspect me for anything, sir, but the want of love, faith, and
duty to you, the bravest, worthiest of mankind. Believe me, I   345
could die for you, sir.

MANLY

Nay, there you lie, sir. Did I not see thee more afraid in the
fight than the chaplain of the ship, or the purser that bought
his place?

FIDELIA

Can he be said to be afraid that ventures to sea with you?   350

342–3 *probation sermons* preached to demonstrate a candidate's fitness
    for church preferment

MANLY

Fie, fie, no more! I shall hate thy flattery worse than thy cowardice, nay, than thy bragging.

FIDELIA

Well, I own then I was afraid, mightily afraid; yet for you I would be afraid again, an hundred times afraid. Dying is ceasing to be afraid, and that I could do sure for you; and   355
you'll believe me one day.   *(Weeps)*

FREEMAN

Poor youth! Believe his eyes, if not his tongue; he seems to speak truth with them.

MANLY

What, does he cry? A pox on't, a maudlin flatterer is as nauseously troublesome as a maudlin drunkard.—No more,   360
you little milksop; do not cry. I'll never make thee afraid again; for of all men, if I had occasion, thou shouldst not be my second; and when I go to sea again, thou shalt venture thy life no more with me.

FIDELIA

Why, will you leave me behind then? *(Aside)* If you would   365
preserve my life, I'm sure you should not.

MANLY

Leave thee behind? Ay, ay; thou art a hopeful youth for the shore only. Here thou wilt live to be cherished by fortune and the great ones, for thou may'st easily come to out-flatter a dull poet, out-lie a coffee-house or gazette writer, out-   370
swear a knight of the post, out-watch a pimp, out-fawn a rook, out-promise a lover, out-rail a wit, and out-brag a sea captain. All this thou canst do because thou'rt a coward, a thing I hate; therefore thou'lt do better with the world than with me, and these are the good courses you must take in the   375
world. There's good advice, at least, at parting; go, and be happy with't.

FIDELIA

Parting, sir? O, let me not hear that dismal word!

MANLY

If my words frighten thee, be gone the sooner; for, to be plain with thee, cowardice and I cannot dwell together.   380

---

367 *hopeful* promising
370 *coffee-house . . . writer* Foreign news was received and translated at the coffee-houses before appearing in the *London Gazette* and other news-sheets.
371 *knight of the post* see 'The Persons', p. 12

FIDELIA

And cruelty and courage never dwelt together sure, sir. Do
not turn me off to shame and misery, for I am helpless and
friendless.

MANLY

Friendless! There are half a score friends for thee then;
(Offers her gold) I leave myself no more. They'll help thee a   385
little. Be gone, go! I must be cruel to thee, if thou call'st it
so, out of pity.

FIDELIA

If you would be cruelly pitiful, sir, let it be with your sword,
not gold.   *(Exit)*

Enter FIRST SAILOR

1 SAILOR

We have, with much ado, turned away two gentlemen who   390
told us forty times over their names were Master Novel and
Major Oldfox.

MANLY

Well, to your post again.   *(Exit* SAILOR*)*
But how come those puppies coupled always together?

FREEMAN

O, the coxcombs keep each other company to show each   395
other, as Novel calls it, or, as Oldfox says, like two knives to
whet one another.

MANLY

And set other people's teeth an edge.

Enter SECOND SAILOR

2 SAILOR

Here is a woman, an't like your honour, scolds and bustles
with us to come in, as much as a seaman's widow at the   400
Navy Office. Her name is Mistress Blackacre.

MANLY

That fiend too!

389 *not* Q1, 0 (and not Q2–8)

---

381 *sure* securely, confidently
398 *an edge* on edge
399 *bustles* scuffles, struggles
400 *seaman's widow* entitled to a lump sum payment of between £2
   and £10, which the Navy Office did not always pay
401 *Navy Office* at Crutched Friars, near Tower Hill; it dealt with all
   Admiralty business

C

FREEMAN

The Widow Blackacre, is it not? That litigious she-petti-
fogger, who is at law and difference with all the world! But
I wish I could make her agree with me in the church; they   405
say she has fifteen hundred pounds a year jointure, and the
care of her son—that is, the destruction of his estate.

MANLY

Her lawyers, attorneys, and solicitors have fifteen hundred
pound a year, whilst she is contented to be poor to make
other people so, for she is as vexatious as her father was, the   410
great attorney, nay, as a dozen Norfolk attorneys, and as
implacable an adversary as a wife suing for alimony or a
parson for his tithes; and she loves an Easter term, or any
term, not as other country ladies do, to come up to be fine,
cuckold their husbands, and take their pleasure; for she has   415
no pleasure but in vexing others, and is usually clothed and
daggled like a bawd in disguise, pursued through alleys by
serjeants. When she is in town she lodges in one of the Inns
of Chancery, where she breeds her son and is herself his
tutoress in law-French; and for her country abode, though   420
she has no estate there, she chooses Norfolk. But bid her
come in, with a pox to her.   *(Exit* SAILOR*)*
She is Olivia's kinswoman, and may make me amends for
her visit by some discourse of that dear woman.

403–4 *pettifogger* dishonest promoter of petty lawsuits
411 *Norfolk attorneys* so numerous and so mischievous their ranks were
    thinned by statute in 1455
413 *Easter term* 'which beginneth always the seventeenth day after
    Easter, and lasteth 27 days' (Chamberlayne, II, 129); the others are
    Trinity, Michaelmas, and Hilary
414 *come up* i.e., to London
417 *daggled* spattered with mud
417 *in disguise* tipsy (?)
418 *serjeants* Court officers empowered to arrest offenders, summon
    witnesses, etc.
418–19 *Inns of Chancery* eight student residences attached to the Inns of
    Court, with some accommodation available to outsiders
419 *breeds* educates
420 *law-French* 'the corrupt variety of Norman French used in English
    law-books' (*OED*)
421 *Norfolk* 'where men are said to *study Law as following the Plough-
    tail* [and] some would perswade us, that they will *enter an action
    for their neighbour's horse but looking over their hedge*' (Thomas
    Fuller, *A History of the Worthies of England,* ed. J. Nichols (1811),
    II, 125–6)

Enter WIDOW BLACKACRE *with a mantle and a green bag, and several papers in the other hand,* JERRY BLACKACRE *her son, in a gown, laden with green bags, following her*

WIDOW
I never had so much to-do with a judge's door-keeper as   425
with yours, but—

MANLY
But the incomparable Olivia, how does she since I went?

WIDOW
Since you went, my suit—

MANLY
Olivia, I say, is she well?

WIDOW
My suit, if you had not returned—   430

MANLY
Damn your suit! How does your cousin Olivia?

WIDOW
My suit, I say, had been quite lost; but now—

MANLY
But now, where is Olivia? In town? For—

WIDOW
For tomorrow we are to have a hearing.

MANLY
Would you'd let me have a hearing today!   435

WIDOW
But why won't you hear me?

MANLY
I am no judge and you talk of nothing but suits; but, pray
tell me, when did you see Olivia?

WIDOW
I am no visitor but a woman of business; or, if I ever visit,
'tis only the Chancery Lane ladies, ladies towards the law, 440
and not any of your lazy, good-for-nothing flirts who cannot
read law-French, though a gallant writ it. But, as I was
telling you, my suit—

MANLY
Damn these impertinent, vexatious people of business, of all
sexes! They are still troubling the world with the tedious 445

424 s.d. *green bag* in which barristers and lawyers carried documents
and papers; cf. '*Green-bag*, a Lawyer' (*B.E.*)
425 *to-do* fuss
440 *Chancery Lane* running from Fleet Street to Holborn, and inhabited
largely by lawyers, whose families perhaps make up the 'ladies towards (i.e., interested in) the law'   445 *still* always

recitals of their lawsuits, and one can no more stop their mouths than a wit's when he talks of himself, or an intelligencer's when he talks of other people.

WIDOW

And a pox of all vexatious, impertinent lovers! They are still perplexing the world with the tedious narrations of their 450
love-suits and discourses of their mistresses. You are as troublesome to a poor widow of business as a young coxcombly rithming lover.

MANLY

And thou art as troublesome to me as a rook to a losing gamester, or a young putter of cases to his mistress and 455
sempstress, who has love in her head for another.

WIDOW

Nay, since you talk of putting of cases and will not hear me speak, hear our Jerry a little; let him put our case to you, for the trial's tomorrow, and since you are my chief witness, I would have your memory refreshed and your judgment 460
informed, that you may not give your evidence improperly. Speak out, child.

JERRY

Yes, forsooth. Hem hem! John-a-Stiles—

MANLY

You may talk, young lawyer, but I shall no more mind you than a hungry judge does a cause after the clock has struck 465
one.

FREEMAN

Nay, you'll find him as peevish too.

WIDOW

No matter.—Jerry, go on.—[To FREEMAN] Do you observe it then, sir, for I think I have seen you in a gown once. Lord, I could hear our Jerry put cases all day long! Mark him, sir. 470

---

453 *rithming* Q1–3 (riming Q4–7; rhiming Q8, 0)

447–8 *intelligencer* (1) informer (2) newsmonger; both meanings are appropriate here
453 *rithming* At this period *rithme, rhythm,* and *rime* (in this sense) were merely spelling variants for, and pronounced the same as, the modern *rhyme.*
455 *putter of cases* law student
463 *John-a-Stiles* John (who dwells) at the stile; an arbitrary name for one of the parties in a legal suit, like the modern John Doe
465–6 *struck one* 'And Wretches hang that Jury-men may Dine' (Pope, *The Rape of the Lock* (1714), III, 22)

JERRY

    John-a-Stiles—no. There are first Fitz, Pere, and Ayle—no,
no: Ayle, Pere, and Fitz. Ayle is seised in fee of Blackacre,
John-a-Stiles disseises Ayle, Ayle makes claim, and the disseisor dies; then the Ayle—no, the Fitz—

WIDOW

    No; the Pere, sirrah.   475

JERRY

    O, the Pere! Ay, the Pere, sir, and the Fitz—no, the Ayle—
no, the Pere and the Fitz, sir, and—

MANLY

    Damn Pere, Mere, and Fitz, sir!

WIDOW

    No, you are out, child.—Hear me, captain, then. There are
Ayle, Pere, and Fitz; Ayle is seised in fee of Blackacre, and   480
being so seised, John-a-Stiles disseises the Ayle, Ayle makes
claim, and the disseisor dies; and then the Pere re-enters—
(to JERRY*)* the Pere, sirrah, the Pere—and the Fitz enters upon
the Pere, and the Ayle brings his writ of disseisin in the *post*,
and the Pere brings his writ of disseisin in the *per*, and—   485

MANLY

    Canst thou hear this stuff, Freeman? I could as soon suffer
a whole noise of flatterers at a great man's levee in a morning; but thou hast servile complacency enough to listen to a

---

485 *per* Q2 (Pere Q1, Q3–8, 0)

471 *Fitz, Pere, and Ayle* Son, Father, and Grandfather, law-French
names used like John-a-Stiles. The case which follows bristles with
problems for a student of law. In outline, Ayle has possession of a
piece of land, Stiles dispossesses him (perhaps on behalf of Pere,
who later *re*-enters), Ayle begins proceedings to recover the land,
Stiles dies (and Ayle's case now collapses if he is suing in a personal action of Ejectment), Pere obtains possession (as abator if a
new claimant, or as Stiles' heir, which is possible despite the implied
relationship between Grandfather and Father if Stiles were, say,
Pere's deceased mother's brother), Fitz ousts Pere, and both Ayle
and Pere sue Fitz for recovery of the land, Ayle by writ of entry
sur disseisin in the *post* (alleging more than two steps between dispossessor and defendant, though he should sue in the *per* and *cui,*
since he alleges Fitz only got entry through Pere who got it
through Stiles who dispossessed Ayle), and Pere by writ of entry in
the *per* (though it should be *in le quibus,* since he alleges Fitz is
the original dispossessor, but that would spoil the pun on *per* and
Pere, which is presumably Wycherley's main point).

479 *out* in error

487 *noise* band, company (usually of musicians)

quibbling statesman in disgrace, nay, and be beforehand with
him in laughing at his dull no-jest. But I— 490

(Offering to go out)

WIDOW

Nay, sir, hold!—Where's the subpœna, Jerry?—I must serve
you, sir. You are required by this to give your testimony—

MANLY

I'll be forsworn, to be revenged on thee.

(Exit MANLY, throwing away the subpœna)

WIDOW

Get you gone, for a lawless companion!—Come, Jerry. I had
almost forgot we were to meet at the master's at three; let 495
us mind our business still, child.

JERRY

Ay, forsooth, e'en so let's.

FREEMAN

Nay madam, now I would beg you to hear me a little, a little
of my business.

WIDOW

I have business of my own calls me away, sir. 500

FREEMAN

My business would prove yours too, dear madam.

WIDOW

Yours would be some sweet business, I warrant. What, 'tis
no Westminster Hall business? Would you have my advice?

FREEMAN

No faith, 'tis a little Westminster Abbey business. I would
have your consent. 505

WIDOW

O fie fie sir, to me such discourse, before my dear minor
there!

JERRY

Ay ay mother, he would be taking livery and seisin of your
jointure by digging the turf. [*Aside*] But I'll watch your
waters, bully, i'fac.—Come away, mother. 510

(Exit JERRY, haling away his mother)

---

489 *quibbling* punning
508 *livery and seisin* i.e., livery of seisin, delivery of possession of lands,
a common law ceremony where 'the Vendor takes . . . a clod of
Earth upon a twig or bough, which he delivers to the Vendee, in
the name of Possession' (Blount); if Freeman takes the livery, the
Widow digs the turf, but Jerry's inaccuracy makes possible the
double entendre
509–10 *watch your waters* keep a sharp eye on you (slang)
510 *i'fac* in faith

Manet FREEMAN. *Enter to him* FIDELIA

FIDELIA

Dear sir, you have pity; beget but some in our captain for
me.

FREEMAN

Where is he?

FIDELIA

Within, swearing as much as he did in the great storm, and
cursing you, and sometimes sinks into calms and sighs, and 515
talks of his Olivia.

FREEMAN

He would never trust me to see her; is she handsome?

FIDELIA

No, if you'll take my word; but I am not a proper judge.

FREEMAN

What is she?

FIDELIA

A gentlewoman, I suppose, but of as mean a fortune as 520
beauty; but her relations would not suffer her to go with
him to the Indies, and his aversion to this side of the world,
together with the late opportunity of commanding the
convoy, would not let him stay here longer, though to enjoy
her. 525

FREEMAN

He loves her mightily then?

FIDELIA

Yes, so well, that the remainder of his fortune (I hear about
five or six thousand pounds) he has left her, in case he had
died by the way or before she could prevail with her friends
to follow him, which he expected she should do; and has left 530
behind him his great bosom friend to be her convoy to him.

FREEMAN

What charms has she for him, if she be not handsome?

FIDELIA

He fancies her, I suppose, the only woman of truth and sincerity in the world.

FREEMAN

No common beauty, I confess. 535

FIDELIA

Or else sure he would not have trusted her with so great a

529 *by the way* on the journey

share of his fortune in his absence: I suppose, since his late
loss, all he has.

FREEMAN

Why, has he left it in her own custody?

FIDELIA

I am told so. 540

FREEMAN

Then he has showed love to her indeed in leaving her, like an
old husband that dies as soon as he has made his wife a good
jointure. But I'll go in to him and speak for you, and know
more from him of his Olivia. *(Exit)*

Manet FIDELIA, *sola*

FIDELIA

His Olivia, indeed, his happy Olivia! 545
Yet she was left behind, when I was with him;
But she was ne'er out of his mind or heart.
She has told him she loved him; I have showed it,
And durst not tell him so till I had done,
Under this habit, such convincing acts 550
Of loving friendship for him, that through it
He first might find out both my sex and love;
And, when I'd had him from his fair Olivia
And this bright world of artful beauties here,
Might then have hoped he would have looked on me 555
Amongst the sooty Indians; and I could,
To choose, there live his wife, where wives are forced
To live no longer when their husbands die;
Nay, what's yet worse, to share 'em whilst they live
With many rival wives. But here he comes, 560
And I must yet keep out of his sight, not
To lose it for ever. *(Exit)*

Enter MANLY *and* FREEMAN

557 *To choose* By choice, If I had my choice
557–60 *there . . . wives* cf. Montaigne, *Essais,* II. xxix (ed. cit., II, 428):
'C'est bien autre chose des femmes Indiennes: . . . estant leur
coustume, aux marys d'avoir plusieurs femmes, et à la plus chere
d'elles de se tuer après son mary'; G. B. Ives translates: 'It is quite
another thing with the Indian women; . . . it being customary with
them for the husband to have many wives, and for the one who is
dearest to kill herself when her husband dies' (ed. cit., II, 954)
562 s.d. (*Exit*) Restoration dramatists did not follow the Elizabethan
practice of beginning a new scene every time the stage is momen-
tarily cleared.

FREEMAN

But, pray, what strange charms has she that could make you
love?

MANLY

Strange charms indeed! She has beauty enough to call in   565
question her wit or virtue, and her form would make a
starved hermit a ravisher; yet her virtue and conduct would
preserve her from the subtle lust of a pampered prelate. She
is so perfect a beauty that art could not better it, nor affectation deform it; yet all this is nothing. Her tongue as well as 570
face ne'er knew artifice, nor ever did her words or looks
contradict her heart. She is all truth, and hates the lying,
masking, daubing world as I do, for which I love her and for
which I think she dislikes not me. For she has often shut out
of her conversation, for mine, the gaudy fluttering parrots of 575
the town, apes and echoes of men only, and refused their
commonplace, pert chat, flattery, and submissions, to be
entertained with my sullen bluntness and honest love. And,
last of all, swore to me, since her parents would not suffer
her to go with me, she would stay behind for no other man,   580
but follow me without their leave, if not to be obtained.
Which oath—

FREEMAN

Did you think she would keep?

MANLY

Yes; for she is not, I tell you, like other women, but can keep
her promise, though she has sworn to keep it. But, that she 585
might the better keep it, I left her the value of five or six
thousand pound, for women's wants are generally their most
importunate solicitors to love or marriage.

FREEMAN

And money summons lovers more than beauty, and aug-
ments but their importunity and their number, so makes it   590
the harder for a woman to deny 'em. For my part, I am for
the French maxim: if you would have your female subjects
loyal, keep 'em poor. But, in short, that your mistress may
not marry, you have given her a portion.

MANLY

She had given me her heart first, and I am satisfied with the 595
security. I can never doubt her truth and constancy.

573 *daubing* painting
575 *conversation* company
577 *submissions* 'acts of deference or homage' (*OED*)
592 *French maxim* unidentified

FREEMAN

It seems you do, since you are fain to bribe it with money.
But how come you to be so diffident of the man that says he
loves you, and not doubt the woman that says it?

MANLY

I should, I confess, doubt the love of any other woman but   600
her, as I do the friendship of any other man but him I have
trusted; but I have such proofs of their faith as cannot
deceive me.

FREEMAN

Cannot!

MANLY

Not but I know that generally no man can be a great enemy   605
but under the name of friend; and if you are a cuckold, it is
your friend only that makes you so, for your enemy is not
admitted to your house; if you are cheated in your fortune,
'tis your friend that does it, for your enemy is not made
your trustee; if your honour or good name be injured, 'tis   610
your friend that does it still, because your enemy is not
believed against you. Therefore I rather choose to go where
honest, downright barbarity is professed; where men devour
one another like generous, hungry lions and tigers, not like
crocodiles; where they think the devil white, of our com-   615
plexion, and I am already so far an Indian. But if your weak
faith doubts this miracle of a woman, come along with me
and believe, and thou wilt find her so handsome that thou,
who art so much my friend, wilt have a mind to lie with her,
and so will not fail to discover what her faith and thine is to   620
me.

When we're in love, the great adversity,
Our friends and mistresses at once we try.   [*Exeunt*]

Finis actus primi

614 *generous* noble, magnanimous
615 *crocodiles* hypocrites; crocodiles were thought to weep while devour-
       ing men
615 *they think the devil white* while Europeans think him black;
       Manly agrees: in England, the devil is a hypocrite in a white mask
623 s.d. [*Exeunt*] At this period, an empty stage indicated the end of an
       act; no curtain fell; after the interval, the scenery was changed in
       full view of the audience to the next location.

Act II, Scene i

OLIVIA's *Lodging*

Enter OLIVIA, ELIZA, LETTICE

OLIVIA

Ah, cousin, what a world 'tis we live in! I am so weary of it.

ELIZA

Truly, cousin, I can find no fault with it, but that we cannot always live in't; for I can never be weary of it.

OLIVIA

O hideous! You cannot be in earnest, sure, when you say you like the filthy world.   5

ELIZA

You cannot be in earnest, sure, when you say you dislike it.

OLIVIA

You are a very censorious creature, I find.

ELIZA

I must confess I think we women as often discover where we love by railing, as men when they lie by their swearing; and the world is but a constant keeping gallant, whom we fail not   10
to quarrel with when anything crosses us, yet cannot part with't for our hearts.

LETTICE

A gallant indeed, madam, whom ladies first make jealous and then quarrel with it for being so; for if by her indiscretion a lady be talked of for a man, she cries presently ' 'Tis a cen-   15
sorious world'; if by her vanity the intrigue be found out, ' 'Tis a prying, malicious world'; if by her over-fondness the gallant proves unconstant, ' 'Tis a false world'; and if by her niggard-liness the chamber-maid tells, ' 'Tis a perfidious world'—but that, I'm sure, your ladyship cannot say of the world yet, as   20
bad as 'tis.

OLIVIA

But I may say ' 'Tis a very impertinent world'. Hold your peace.—And, cousin, if the world be a gallant, 'tis such an one as is my aversion. Pray name it no more.

8 *discover* reveal
10 *keeping gallant* lover who maintains his mistress
15 *talked of for a man* linked in gossip with some particular man

ELIZA

But is it possible the world, which has such variety of charms   25
for other women, can have none for you? Let's see. First,
what d'ye think of dressing and fine clothes?

OLIVIA

Dressing? Fie fie, 'tis my aversion. [*To* LETTICE] But come
hither, you dowdy; methinks you might have opened this
tour better. O hideous! I cannot suffer it! D'ye see how it   30
sits?

ELIZA

Well enough, cousin, if dressing be your aversion.

OLIVIA

'Tis so; and for variety of rich clothes, they are more my
aversion.

LETTICE

Ay, 'tis because your ladyship wears 'em too long; for indeed   35
a gown, like a gallant, grows one's aversion by having too
much of it.

OLIVIA

Insatiable creature! I'll be sworn I have had this not above
three days, cousin, and within this month have made some
six more.   40

ELIZA

Then your aversion to 'em is not altogether so great.

OLIVIA

Alas! 'Tis for my woman only I wear 'em, cousin.

LETTICE

If it be for me only, madam, pray do not wear 'em.

ELIZA

But what d'ye think of visits, balls—

OLIVIA

O, I detest 'em.   45

ELIZA

Of plays?

OLIVIA

I abominate 'em. Filthy, obscene, hideous things!

29 *dowdy* a noun
30 *tour* artificial curls worn on the forehead
39 *made* i.e., had made; on 1 May 1669 Pepys writes 'the stuff suit I
made the last year'

ELIZA

What say you to masquerading in the winter, and Hyde Park
in the summer?

OLIVIA

Insipid pleasures I taste not.   50

ELIZA

Nay, if you are for more solid pleasure, what think you of a
rich young husband?

OLIVIA

O horrid! Marriage! What a pleasure you have found out!
I nauseate it of all things.

LETTICE

But what does your ladyship think then of a liberal, hand-   55
some young lover?

OLIVIA

A handsome young fellow, you impudent? Be gone, out of
my sight! Name a handsome young fellow to me! Foh, a
hideous, handsome young fellow I abominate.   (*Spits*)

ELIZA

Indeed! But let's see; will nothing please you? What d'ye   60
think of the court?

OLIVIA

How? The court, the court, cousin! My aversion, my aversion, my aversion of all aversions.

ELIZA

How? The court! Where—

OLIVIA

Where sincerity is a quality as out of fashion and as   65
unprosperous as bashfulness. I could not laugh at a quibble,
though it were a fat privy counsellor's; nor praise a lord's
ill verses, though I were myself the subject; nor an old lady's
young looks, though I were her woman; nor sit to a vain
young simile-maker, though he flattered me. In short, I could 70
not gloat upon a man when he comes into a room, and laugh

---

48 *Hyde Park* 'the promenade of London . . . the rendez-vous of
   magnificence and beauty: every one, therefore, who had either
   sparkling eyes, or a splendid equipage, constantly repaired thither'
   (Anthony Hamilton, *Memoirs of the Count de Grammont* (1926),
   p. 171)
55 *liberal* (1) generous (2) licentious
59 s.d. (*Spits*) to avert a threatened evil; Dryden's Friar Dominic does
   so in *The Spanish Fryar* (1680), when hypocritically disclaiming his
   interest in 'a sweet young girl' (IV. i)
70 *simile-maker* portrait-painter
71 *gloat* 'cast amorous or admiring glances' (*OED*)

at him when he goes out. I cannot rail at the absent to flatter
the standers-by; I—

ELIZA

Well, but railing now is so common that 'tis no more malice,
but the fashion; and the absent think they are no more the   75
worse for being railed at than the present think they're the
better for being flattered; and for the court—

OLIVIA

Nay, do not defend the court, for you'll make me rail at it,
like a trusting citizen's widow.

ELIZA

Or like a Holborn lady, who could not get into the last ball   80
or was out of countenance in the drawing-room the last
Sunday of her appearance there. For none rail at the court
but those who cannot get into it or else who are ridiculous
when they are there; and I shall suspect you were laughed at
when you were last there or would be a maid of honour.   85

OLIVIA

I, a maid of honour! To be a maid of honour were yet of all
things my aversion.

ELIZA

In what sense am I to understand you? But, in fine, by the
word 'aversion' I'm sure you dissemble, for I never knew
woman yet that used it who did not. Come, our tongues belie   90
our hearts more than our pocket-glasses do our faces; but
methinks we ought to leave off dissembling, since 'tis grown
of no use to us; for all wise observers understand us nowadays as they do dreams, almanacs, and Dutch gazettes, by
the contrary; and a man no more believes a woman when   95
she says she has an aversion for him, than when she says
she'll cry out.

OLIVIA

O filthy, hideous! Peace, cousin, or your discourse will be
my aversion; and you may believe me.

76 *they're* Q2b–8, 0 (they are Q1–2a)

---

79 *trusting citizen* credit-giving tradesman, presumably ruined by bad
debts
80 *Holborn* a main highway into the city, running from Tottenham
Court Road to Newgate; an unfashionable address
81 *the drawing-room* The King and Queen held large receptions in
their withdrawing-rooms at Whitehall; Evelyn saw 'innumerable'
visitors 'of the first sort' there on 2 May 1671.
85 *maid of honour* unmarried lady attending upon the Queen
94 *Dutch gazettes* especially unreliable, since they reported matters
from a viewpoint hostile to England

ELIZA

Yes, for if anything be a woman's aversion, 'tis plain dealing 100
from another woman; and perhaps that's your quarrel to the
world, for that will talk, as your woman says.

OLIVIA

Talk not of me, sure; for what men do I converse with, what
visits do I admit?

Enter BOY

BOY

Here's the gentleman to wait upon you, madam. 105

OLIVIA

On me! You little, unthinking fop, d'ye know what you say?

BOY

Yes, madam; 'tis the gentleman that comes every day to you,
who—

OLIVIA

Hold your peace, you heedless little animal, and get you
gone. *(Exit* BOY) 110
This country boy, cousin, takes my dancing-master, tailor, or
the spruce milliner for visitors.

LETTICE

No, madam; 'tis Master Novel, I'm sure, by his talking so
loud. I know his voice too, madam.

OLIVIA

You know nothing, you buffle-headed, stupid creature, you; 115
you would make my cousin believe I receive visits. But if it
be Master—what did you call him?

LETTICE

Master Novel, madam; he that—

OLIVIA

Hold your peace, I'll hear no more of him. But if it be your
Master—(I can't think of his name again), I suppose he has 120
followed my cousin hither.

ELIZA

No, cousin, I will not rob you of the honour of the visit; 'tis
to you, cousin, for I know him not.

OLIVIA

Nor did I ever hear of him before, upon my honour, cousin.
Besides, han't I told you that visits and the business of visits, 125
flattery and detraction, are my aversion? D'ye think then I

112 *milliner* man selling cutlery, haberdashery, and fancy goods
115 *buffle-headed* dim-witted

would admit such a coxcomb as he is, who rather than not
rail, will rail at the dead, whom none speak ill of; and rather
than not flatter, will flatter the poets of the age, whom none
will flatter; who affects novelty as much as the fashion, and   130
is as fantastical as changeable, and as well known as the
fashion; who likes nothing but what is new, nay, would
choose to have his friend or his title a new one. In fine, he is
my aversion.

ELIZA

I find you do know him, cousin; at least, have heard of him.   135

OLIVIA

Yes, now I remember, I have heard of him.

ELIZA

Well; but since he is such a coxcomb, for heaven's sake let
him not come up.—Tell him, Mistress Lettice, your lady is
not within.

OLIVIA

No, Lettice, tell him my cousin is here, and that he may come   140
up;—for, notwithstanding I detest the sight of him, you may
like his conversation; and though I would use him scurvily,
I will not be rude to you in my own lodging. Since he has
followed you hither, let him come up, I say.

ELIZA

Very fine! Pray let him go to the devil, I say, for me; I know   145
him not, nor desire it.—Send him away, Mistress
Lettice.

OLIVIA

Upon my word, she shan't. I must disobey your commands
to comply with your desires.—Call him up, Lettice.

ELIZA

Nay, I'll swear she shall not stir on that errand.   150

(Holds LETTICE*)*

OLIVIA

Well then, I'll call him myself for you, since you will have
it so. *(Calls out at the door)* Master Novel, sir, sir!

Enter NOVEL

NOVEL

Madam, I beg your pardon; perhaps you were busy. I did
not think you had company with you.

---

131 *fantastical* (1) capricious in opinion (2) foppish in dress
145 *for me* as far as I'm concerned
152 s.d. *door* i.e., one of the permanent doors in the proscenium arch

ELIZA *(Aside)*
  Yet he comes to me, cousin!   155
OLIVIA
  Chairs there!   [*Exit* LETTICE]

[*Enter* SERVANTS, *who place chairs and withdraw.*] *They sit*

NOVEL
  Well, but madam, d'ye know whence I come now?
OLIVIA
  From some melancholy place, I warrant, sir, since they have
  lost your good company.
ELIZA
  So.   160
NOVEL
  From a place where they have treated me at dinner with so
  much civility and kindness, a pox on 'em, that I could
  hardly get away to you, dear madam.
OLIVIA
  You have a way with you so new and obliging, sir.
ELIZA *(Apart to* OLIVIA*)*
  You hate flattery, cousin!   165
NOVEL
  Nay, faith, madam, d'ye think my way new? Then you are
  obliging, madam. I must confess I hate imitation, to do
  anything like other people; all that know me do me the
  honour to say I am an original, faith. But as I was saying,
  madam, I have been treated today with all the ceremony and   170
  kindness imaginable at my Lady Autumn's; but the nauseous
  old woman at the upper end of her table—
OLIVIA
  Revives the old Grecian custom of serving in a death's head
  with their banquets.
NOVEL
  Ha ha! Fine, just, i'faith; nay, and new. 'Tis like eating with 175

---

156 s.d. [*Exit* LETTICE] Unless her re-entry at 675 is an error, she must
    exit sometime before; here is her best opportunity.
173 *serving in a death's head* This is not a Greek custom; Herodotus
    says the Egyptians paraded a dummy corpse at their feasts, as a
    memento mori (II. 78), but Wycherley probably found it in Mon-
    taigne, *Essais*, I, xx (ed. cit., I, 91): 'les Egyptiens, après leurs
    festins, faisoient presenter aux assistans une grand'image de la mort
    par un qui leur crioit: "Boy et t'esjouy, car, mort, tu seras tel" '.
174 *banquets* sweetmeats, fruit, and wine served as dessert

the ghost in *The Libertine*; she would frighten a man from
her dinner with her hollow invitations, and spoil one's
stomach—

OLIVIA

To meat or women. I detest her hollow, cherry cheeks. She
looks like an old coach new painted, affecting an unseemly   180
smugness whilst she is ready to drop in pieces.

ELIZA *(Apart to* OLIVIA*)*

You hate detraction I see, cousin!

NOVEL

But the silly old fury, whilst she affects to look like a woman
of this age, talks—

OLIVIA

Like one of the last, and as passionately as an old courtier   185
who has outlived his office.

NOVEL

Yes, madam; but pray let me give you her character. Then
she never counts her age by the years, but—

OLIVIA

By the masques she has lived to see.

NOVEL

Nay then, madam, I see you think a little harmless railing   190
too great a pleasure for any but yourself, and therefore I've
done.

OLIVIA

Nay, faith, you shall tell me who you had there at dinner.

NOVEL

If you would hear me, madam.

OLIVIA

Most patiently. Speak, sir.   195

NOVEL

Then we had her daughter—

OLIVIA

Ay, her daughter, the very disgrace to good clothes, which
she always wears but to heighten her deformity, not mend it;
for she is still most splendidly, gallantly, ugly, and looks like
an ill piece of daubing in a rich frame.   200

---

176 *The Libertine* Novel's memory of Shadwell's play (1675) is blurred;
  only Don John's man is frightened when the statue of his master's
  victim comes to dinner in Act IV, though both refuse to drink a
  glass of blood when the ghost returns hospitality in Act V.
181 *smugness* smartness

NOVEL

So! But have you done with her, madam? And can you
spare her to me a little now?

OLIVIA

Ay ay, sir.

NOVEL

Then she is like—

OLIVIA

She is, you'd say, like a city bride: the greater fortune, but 205
not the greater beauty, for her dress.

NOVEL

Well. Yet have you done, madam? Then she—

OLIVIA

Then she bestows as unfortunately on her face all the graces
in fashion, as the languishing eye, the hanging or pouting lip;
but as the fool is never more provoking than when he aims 210
at wit, the ill-favoured of our sex are never more nauseous
than when they would be beauties, adding to their natural
deformity the artificial ugliness of affectation.

ELIZA

So, cousin, I find one may have a collection of all one's
acquaintances' pictures as well at your house as at Master 215
Lely's, only the difference is there we find 'em much hand-
somer than they are and like, here much uglier and like; and
you are the first of the profession of picture-drawing I ever
knew without flattery.

OLIVIA

I draw after the life; do nobody wrong, cousin. 220

ELIZA

No, you hate flattery and detraction!

OLIVIA

But, Master Novel, who had you besides at dinner?

NOVEL

Nay, the devil take me if I tell you, unless you will allow
me the privilege of railing in my turn. But, now I think on't,
the women ought to be your province, as the men are mine; 225
and you must know we had him whom—

OLIVIA

Him, whom—

205–6 *city . . . dress* another attack on merchants with more money than
taste
216 *Lely* see Prologue 30; Lely was knighted on 11 January 1679/80

NOVEL

What? Invading me already? And giving the character
before you know the man?

ELIZA

No, that is not fair, though it be usual.   230

OLIVIA

I beg your pardon, Master Novel; pray go on.

NOVEL

Then, I say, we had that familiar coxcomb, who is at home
wheresoe'er he comes.

OLIVIA

Ay, that fool—

NOVEL

Nay then, madam, your servant. I'm gone. Taking a fool out   235
of one's mouth is worse than taking the bread out of one's
mouth.

OLIVIA

I've done. Your pardon, Master Novel; pray proceed.

NOVEL

I say, the rogue, that he may be the only wit in company,
will let nobody else talk, and—   240

OLIVIA

Ay, those fops who love to talk all themselves are of all
things my aversion.

NOVEL

Then you'll let me speak, madam, sure. The rogue, I say, will
force his jest upon you, and I hate a jest that's forced upon
a man as much as a glass.   245

ELIZA

Why, I hope, sir, he does not expect a man of your temper-
ance in jesting should do him reason?

NOVEL

What, interruption from this side too! I must then—
                    (Offers to rise. OLIVIA *holds him)*

OLIVIA

No, sir.—You must know, cousin, that fop he means, though
he talks only to be commended, will not give you leave to   250
do't.

NOVEL

But, madam—

247 *do him reason* keep pace with him in drinking
248 s.d. *Offers* Attempts

OLIVIA

He a wit! Hang him, he's only an adopter of straggling jests
and fatherless lampoons, by the credit of which he eats at
good tables and so, like the barren beggar-woman, lives by   255
borrowed children.

NOVEL

Madam—

OLIVIA

And never was author of anything but his news; but that is
still all his own.

NOVEL

Madam, pray—   260

OLIVIA

An eternal babbler, and makes no more use of his ears than
a man that sits at a play by his mistress or in fop-corner.
He's, in fine, a base, detracting fellow, and is my aversion.—
But who else prithee, Master Novel, was there with you?
Nay, you shan't stir.   265

NOVEL

I beg your pardon, madam; I cannot stay in any place where
I'm not allowed a little Christian liberty of railing.

OLIVIA

Nay, prithee, Master Novel, stay; and though you should rail
at me, I would hear you with patience. Prithee, who else was
there with you?   270

NOVEL

Your servant, madam.

OLIVIA

Nay, prithee tell us, Master Novel, prithee do.

NOVEL

We had nobody else.

OLIVIA

Nay, faith, I know you had. Come, my Lord Plausible was
there too, who is, cousin, a—   275

ELIZA

You need not tell me what he is, cousin, for I know him to
be a civil, good-natured, harmless gentleman, that speaks well
of all the world, and is always in good humour, and—

262 *fop-corner* the foremost benches of the pit, where wits-about-town
  congregated; Otway's *Friendship in Fashion* (1678) refers to 'ev'ry
  trim amorous twiring Fop of the Corner, that comes thither to make
  a noise, hear no Play, and show himself' (V. 520–2)
271 *Your servant, madam* a polite way of expressing disagreement

OLIVIA

Hold, cousin, hold! I hate detraction, but I must tell you,
cousin, his civility is cowardice, his good nature want of wit,   280
and has neither courage or sense to rail; and for his being
always in humour, 'tis because he is never dissatisfied with
himself. In fine, he is my aversion, and I never admit his
visits beyond my hall.

NOVEL

No, he visit you! Damn him, cringing, grinning rogue! If I   285
should see him coming up to you, I would make bold to
kick him down again.—Ha!

Enter my LORD PLAUSIBLE

My dear lord, your most humble servant.
                              (Rises and salutes PLAUSIBLE *and kisses him)*
ELIZA *(Aside)*

So! I find kissing and railing succeed each other with the
angry men as well as with the angry women; and their   290
quarrels are like love-quarrels, since absence is the only cause
of them, for as soon as the man appears again, they are over.

LORD PLAUSIBLE

Your most faithful, humble servant, generous Master Novel;
—and, madam, I am your eternal slave and kiss your fair
hands, which I had done sooner, according to your com-   295
mands, but—

OLIVIA

No excuses, my lord.

ELIZA *(Apart [to* OLIVIA*])*

What, you sent for him then, cousin?

NOVEL *(Aside)*

Ha! invited!

OLIVIA

I know you must divide yourself, for your good company is   300
too general a good to be engrossed by any particular friend.

LORD PLAUSIBLE

O Lord, madam, my company! Your most obliged, faithful,
humble servant. But I could have brought you good company
indeed, for I parted at your door with two of the worthiest,
bravest men—   305

OLIVIA

Who were they, my lord?

---

288 s.d. *kisses him* 'Lord, what a filthy trick these men have got of kiss-
    ing one another' (Etherege, *The Man of Mode* (1676), I. 69–70)
294–5 *kiss your fair hands* a polite greeting, not necessarily acted upon

NOVEL

Who do you call the worthiest, bravest men, pray?

LORD PLAUSIBLE

O the wisest, bravest gentlemen! Men of such honour and
virtue! Of such good qualities! Ah!

ELIZA *(Aside)*

This is a coxcomb that speaks ill of all people a different 310
way, and libels everybody with dull praise, and commonly
in the wrong place; so makes his panegyrics abusive lampoons.

OLIVIA

But pray let me know who they were.

LORD PLAUSIBLE

Ah! Such patterns of heroic virtue! Such— 315

NOVEL

Well, but who the devil were they?

LORD PLAUSIBLE

The honour of our nation, the glory of our age! Ah, I could
dwell a twelvemonth on their praise, which indeed I might
spare by telling their names: Sir John Current and Sir
Richard Court-Title. 320

NOVEL

Court-Title! Ha ha!

OLIVIA

And Sir John Current! Why will you keep such a wretch
company, my lord?

LORD PLAUSIBLE

Oh, madam, seriously, you are a little too severe, for he is a
man of unquestioned reputation in everything. 325

OLIVIA

Yes, because he endeavours only with the women to pass for
a man of courage, and with the bullies for a wit, with the
wits for a man of business, and with the men of business for
a favourite at court, and at court for good city security.

NOVEL

And for Sir Richard, he— 330

LORD PLAUSIBLE

He loves your choice, picked company, persons that—

OLIVIA

He loves a lord indeed, but—

NOVEL

Pray, dear madam, let me have but a bold stroke or two at
his picture. He loves a lord, as you say, though—

OLIVIA

Though he borrowed his money and ne'er paid him again. 335

NOVEL

And would bespeak a place three days before at the back-end of a lord's coach to Hyde Park.

LORD PLAUSIBLE

Nay, i'faith, i'faith, you are both too severe.

OLIVIA

Then to show yet more his passion for quality, he makes love to that fulsome coach-load of honour, my Lady Goodly, 340 for he is always at her lodging.

LORD PLAUSIBLE

Because it is the conventicle gallant, the meeting-house of all the fair ladies and glorious, superfine beauties of the town.

NOVEL

Very fine ladies! There's first—

OLIVIA

Her honour, as fat as an hostess. 345

LORD PLAUSIBLE

She is something plump indeed, a goodly, comely, graceful person.

NOVEL

Then there's my Lady Frances—what d'ye call 'er?—as ugly—

OLIVIA

As a citizen's lawfully begotten daughter. 350

LORD PLAUSIBLE

She has wit in abundance, and the handsomest heel, elbow, and tip of an ear you ever saw.

NOVEL

Heel and elbow! Ha ha! And there's my Lady Betty, you know—

OLIVIA

As sluttish and slatternly as an Irishwoman bred in France. 355

LORD PLAUSIBLE

Ah, all she has hangs with a loose air, indeed, and becoming negligence.

ELIZA

You see all faults with lover's eyes, I find, my lord.

---

342 *meeting-house* Plausible's non-conformist imagery casts doubt upon the social cachet of Lady Goodly's polished assembly or 'conventicle gallant'.

LORD PLAUSIBLE

Ah, madam, your most obliged, faithful, humble servant to command.—But you can say nothing, sure, against the super-   360
fine Mistress—

OLIVIA

I know who you mean. She is as censorious and detracting a jade as a superannuated sinner.

LORD PLAUSIBLE

She has a smart way of raillery, 'tis confessed.

NOVEL

And then, for Mistress Grideline—   365

LORD PLAUSIBLE

She, I'm sure, is—

OLIVIA

One that never spoke ill of anybody, 'tis confessed; for she is as silent in conversation as a country lover, and no better company than a clock or a weather-glass; for if she sounds, 'tis but once an hour, to put you in mind of the time of day   370
or tell you 'twill be cold or hot, rain or snow.

LORD PLAUSIBLE

Ah, poor creature! She's extremely good and modest.

NOVEL

And for Mistress Bridlechin, she's—

OLIVIA

As proud as a churchman's wife.

LORD PLAUSIBLE

She's a woman of great spirit and honour, and will not make   375
herself cheap, 'tis true.

NOVEL

Then Mistress Hoyden, that calls all people by their sur-
names, and is—

OLIVIA

As familiar a duck—

NOVEL

As an actress in the tiring-room. There I was once before-   380
hand with you, madam.

371 *or tell* Q2–8 (or to tell Q1, 0)

---

365 *Grideline* greyish pink; perhaps chosen here to suggest an unhealthy complexion, like Sheridan's Miss Sallow in *The School for Scandal* (1777, II. ii)
377 *Hoyden* type name for a 'boisterous noisy girl, a romp' (*OED*)
380 *tiring-room* dressing-room, where actresses often entertained gallants

LORD PLAUSIBLE

Mistress Hoyden! A poor, affable, good-natured soul! But
the divine Mistress Trifle comes thither too; sure, her beauty,
virtue, and conduct you can say nothing to.

OLIVIA

No?   385

NOVEL

No?—Pray let me speak, madam.

OLIVIA

First, can anyone be called beautiful that squints?

LORD PLAUSIBLE

Her eyes languish a little, I own.

NOVEL

Languish! Ha ha!

OLIVIA

Languish! Then, for her conduct, she was seen at *The*   390
Country Wife after the first day. There's for you, my lord.

LORD PLAUSIBLE

But, madam, she was not seen to use her fan all the play
long, turn aside her head, or by a conscious blush discover
more guilt than modesty.

OLIVIA

Very fine! Then you think a woman modest that sees the   395
hideous *Country Wife* without blushing or publishing her
detestation of it? D'ye hear him, cousin?

ELIZA

Yes, and am, I must confess, something of his opinion, and
think that as an over-captious fool at a play, by endeavouring
to show the author's want of wit, exposes his own to more   400
censure, so may a lady call her own modesty in question by
publicly cavilling with the poet's; for all those grimaces of
honour and artificial modesty disparage a woman's real
virtue as much as the use of white and red does the natural
complexion, and you must use very, very little if you would   405
have it thought your own.

---

399 *over-captious* Q2–8 (over-conscious Q1, 0)

384 *conduct* discretion
391 *the first day* The first recorded performance of Wycherley's comedy
    was given at Drury Lane on 12 January 1675; later audiences knew
    the play's reputation for obscenity in advance.
393 *conscious* knowing
404 *white and red* cosmetics for the face and cheeks

OLIVIA

Then you would have a woman of honour with passive looks, ears, and tongue undergo all the hideous obscenity she hears at nasty plays?

ELIZA

Truly, I think a woman betrays her want of modesty by 410 showing it publicly in a playhouse, as much as a man does his want of courage by a quarrel there, for the truly modest and stout say least and are least exceptious, especially in public.

OLIVIA

O hideous! Cousin, this cannot be your opinion; but you are 415 one of those who have the confidence to pardon the filthy play.

ELIZA

Why, what is there of ill in't, say you?

OLIVIA

O fie fie fie, would you put me to the blush anew, call all the blood into my face again? But to satisfy you then; first, the 420 clandestine obscenity in the very name of Horner.

ELIZA

Truly, 'tis so hidden I cannot find it out, I confess.

OLIVIA

O horrid! Does it not give you the rank conception or image of a goat, a town-bull, or a satyr? Nay, what is yet a filthier image than all the rest, that of an eunuch?   425

ELIZA

What then? I can think of a goat, a bull, or satyr without any hurt.

OLIVIA

Ay; but cousin, one cannot stop there.

ELIZA

I can, cousin.

OLIVIA

O no, for when you have those filthy creatures in your head 430 once, the next thing you think is what they do; as their defiling of honest men's beds and couches, rapes upon sleep-

---

409 *nasty* indecent
413 *exceptious* captious, easily offended
421 *Horner* i.e., cuckold-maker; by feigning impotence, Horner gains ready access to eager wives without sullying their reputations or arousing their husbands' jealousy
424 *town-bull* a bull communally owned by the cow-keepers of a village; hence 'one that rides all the Women he meets' (*B.E.*)

ing and waking country virgins under hedges and on haycocks; nay farther—

ELIZA

Nay, no farther, cousin; we have enough of your comment   435
on the play, which will make me more ashamed than the
play itself.

OLIVIA

O, believe me, 'tis a filthy play; and you may take my word
for a filthy play as soon as another's. But the filthiest thing
in that play, or any other play, is—   440

ELIZA

Pray keep it to yourself, if it be so.

OLIVIA

No, faith, you shall know it; I'm resolved to make you out
of love with the play. I say the lewdest, filthiest thing is his
china; nay, I will never forgive the beastly author his china.
He has quite taken away the reputation of poor china itself,   445
and sullied the most innocent and pretty furniture of a lady's
chamber, insomuch that I was fain to break all my defiled
vessels. You see I have none left; nor you, I hope.

ELIZA

You'll pardon me; I cannot think the worse of my china for
that of the playhouse.   450

OLIVIA

Why, you will not keep any now, sure! 'Tis now as unfit an
ornament for a lady's chamber as the pictures that come
from Italy and other hot countries, as appears by their nudities, which I always cover or scratch out, wheresoe'er I find
'em. But china! Out upon't, filthy china, nasty, debauched   455
china!

ELIZA

All this will not put me out of conceit with china nor the
play, which is acted today, or another of the same beastly
author's, as you call him, which I'll go see.   [Going]

433–4 *haycocks* conical heaps of hay in the field
444 *china* Horner and Lady Fidget retire on pretence of his giving her a
piece of china; when she emerges later with a roll-wagon, Mistress
Squeamish demands china too, but Horner confesses he has 'none
left now' (IV. iii, 187)
446 *furniture* ornaments
452–3 *pictures . . . Italy* pornographic drawings after Giulio Romano's
illustrations to Aretino's *Sonnetti lussoriosi*
457 *put me out of conceit* make me dissatisfied

OLIVIA

You will not, sure! Nay, you shan't venture your reputation   460
by going, and mine by leaving me alone with two men here.
(Pulls her back) Nay, you'll disoblige me for ever if—

ELIZA

I stay.—Your servant.   *(Exit* ELIZA*)*

OLIVIA

Well.—But my lord, though you justify everybody, you
cannot in earnest uphold so beastly a writer, whose ink is so   465
smutty, as one may say.

LORD PLAUSIBLE

Faith, I dare swear the poor man did not think to disoblige
the ladies by any amorous, soft, passionate, luscious saying
in his play.

OLIVIA

Foy, my lord.—But what think you, Master Novel, of the   470
play, though I know you are a friend to all that are new?

NOVEL

Faith, madam, I must confess the new plays would not be the
worse for my advice, but I could never get the silly rogues,
the poets, to mind what I say. But I'll tell you what counsel
I gave the surly fool you speak of.   475

OLIVIA

What was't?

NOVEL

Faith, to put his play into rithme; for rithme, you know,
often makes mystical nonsense pass with the critics for wit,
and a double-meaning saying with the ladies for soft, tender,
and moving passion. But now I talk of passion, I saw your   480
old lover this morning—Captain—   *(Whispers)*

Enter CAPTAIN MANLY, FREEMAN, *and* FIDELIA *standing behind*

OLIVIA

Whom? Nay, you need not whisper.

MANLY

We are luckily got hither unobserved.—How! In a close
conversation with these supple rascals, the outcasts of sempstresses' shops!   485

468 *luscious* lascivious
470 *Foy* Faith (from French *foi*)
477 *rithme* rhyme (see I. 453); the fitness of rhyme for serious plays was
    keenly debated at this time, most memorably in Dryden's *Of
    Dramatic Poesy* (1668), but only Novel could suggest using rhyme
    for a contemporary comedy like *The Country Wife*

FREEMAN

Faith, pardon her, captain, that, since she could no longer be
entertained with your manly bluntness and honest love, she
takes up with the pert chat and commonplace flattery of
these fluttering parrots of the town, apes and echoes of men
only. 490

MANLY

Do not you, sir, play the echo too, mock me, dally with my
own words, and show yourself as impertinent as they are.

FREEMAN

Nay, captain—

FIDELIA

Nay, lieutenant, do not excuse her; methinks she looks very
kindly upon 'em both, and seems to be pleased with what 495
that fool there says to her.

MANLY

You lie, sir; and hold your peace, that I may not be provoked
to give you a worse reply.

OLIVIA

Manly returned, d'ye say? And is he safe?

NOVEL

My lord saw him too. Hark you, my lord. 500

(Whispers to PLAUSIBLE*)*

MANLY *(Aside)*

She yet seems concerned for my safety, and perhaps they are
admitted now here but for their news of me; for intelligence
indeed is the common passport of nauseous fools when they
go their round of good tables and houses.

OLIVIA

I heard of his fighting only, without particulars, and confess 505
I always loved his brutal courage, because it made me hope
it might rid me of his more brutal love.

MANLY *(Apart)*

What's that?

OLIVIA

But is he at last returned, d'ye say, unhurt?

NOVEL

Ay, faith, without doing his business; for the rogue has been 510

486–90 *Faith . . . only* Freeman recalls, almost accurately, Manly's
speech at I. 574–8.
502 *intelligence* information, news
510 *doing his business* ruining or killing himself

these two years pretending to a wooden leg, which he would take from fortune as kindly as the staff of a marshal of France, and rather read his name in a gazette—

OLIVIA

Than in the entail of a good estate.

MANLY *(Aside)*

So!	515

NOVEL

I have an ambition, I must confess, of losing my heart before such a fair enemy as yourself, madam; but that silly rogues should be ambitious of losing their arms, and—

OLIVIA

Looking like a pair of compasses.

NOVEL

But he has no use of his arms but to set 'em on kimbow, for	520
he never pulls off his hat, at least not to me, I'm sure; for you must know, madam, he has a fanatical hatred to good company. He can't abide me.

LORD PLAUSIBLE

O, be not so severe to him as to say he hates good company, for I assure you he has a great respect, esteem, and kindness	525
for me.

MANLY [*Aside*]

That kind, civil rogue has spoken yet ten thousand times worse of me than t'other.

OLIVIA

Well, if he be returned, Master Novel, then shall I be pestered again with his boisterous sea-love, have my alcove smell	530
like a cabin, my chamber perfumed with his tarpaulin brandenburgh, and hear volleys of brandy sighs, enough to make a fog in one's room. Foh, I hate a lover that smells like Thames Street!

511 *pretending* aspiring
512–13 *marshal of France* 'a Title only, without either pension or command' (*OED*, citing Botero's *The World*, tr. R. Johnson (1630), p. 157)
513 *gazette* The *London Gazette* published special supplements giving news of battles during the Dutch wars.
520 *on kimbow* a-kimbo
532 *brandenburgh* a long loose overcoat reaching to the calf; 'it serves to wrap me up, after the Fatigue of a Ball' (Etherege, *The Man of Mode* (1676), IV. ii, 110–11)
534 *Thames Street* running along the north bank of the river from Blackfriars to the Tower; it contained Billingsgate fish market

MANLY

(Aside) I can bear no longer, and need her no more. [*To*   535
OLIVIA] But since you have these two pulvilio boxes, these
essence bottles, this pair of musk-cats here, I hope I may
venture to come yet nearer you.

OLIVIA

Overheard us, then?

NOVEL *(Aside)*

I hope he heard me not.   540

LORD PLAUSIBLE

Most noble and heroic captain, your most obliged, faithful,
humble servant.

NOVEL

Dear tar, thy humble servant.

MANLY

Away!—Madam.

(Thrusts NOVEL *and* PLAUSIBLE *on each side)*

OLIVIA

Nay, I think I have fitted you for listening.   545

MANLY

You have fitted me for believing you could not be fickle
though you were young, could not dissemble love though
'twas your interest, nor be vain though you were handsome,
nor break your promise though to a parting lover, nor abuse
your best friend though you had wit; but I take not your   550
contempt of me worse than your esteem or civility for these
things here, though you know 'em.

NOVEL

Things!

LORD PLAUSIBLE

Let the captain rally a little.

MANLY

Yes, things! *(Coming up to* NOVEL) Canst thou be angry,   555
thou thing?

NOVEL

No, since my lord says you speak in raillery; for though

---

544 s.d. (*Thrusts . . . side*) Q1 prints this after Olivia's next speech, so it
could apply to her or Manly.
548 *be* Q4–8, 0 (be in Q1–3)

---

535 *bear* intransitive
536 *pulvilio* perfumed powder for dressing wigs
537 *musk-cats* animals secreting musk, the basis of many perfumes
545 *fitted you* paid you back

your sea-raillery be something rough, yet I confess we use
one another to as bad every day at Locket's, and never
quarrel for the matter.   560

LORD PLAUSIBLE

Nay, noble captain, be not angry with him. A word with you,
I beseech you.   (*Whispers to* MANLY)

OLIVIA *(Aside)*

Well, we women, like the rest of the cheats of the world,
when our cullies or creditors have found us out and will or
can trust no longer, pay debts and satisfy obligations with a 565
quarrel, the kindest present a man can make to his mistress,
when he can make no more presents; for oftentimes in love,
as at cards, we are forced to play foul only to give over the
game, and use our lovers like the cards: when we can get no
more by 'em, throw 'em up in a pet upon the first dispute.   570

MANLY

My lord, all that you have made me know by your whisper-
ing, which I knew not before, is that you have a stinking
breath. There's a secret for your secret.

LORD PLAUSIBLE

Pshaw, pshaw!

MANLY

But madam, tell me, pray, [*Indicating* NOVEL] what was't   575
about this spark could take you? Was it the merit of his
fashionable impudence, the briskness of his noise, the wit of
his laugh, his judgment or fancy in his garniture? Or was it
a well-trimmed glove, or the scent of it that charmed you?

NOVEL

Very well, sir.—'Gad, these sea-captains make nothing of   580
dressing.—But let me tell you, sir, a man by his dress, as
much as by anything, shows his wit and judgment; nay, and
his courage too.

FREEMAN

How his courage, Master Novel?

NOVEL

Why, for example, by red breeches, tucked-up hair or peruke,   585
a greasy broad belt, and nowadays a short sword.

---

558 *use* accustom
559 *Locket's* an expensive eating-house near Charing Cross
578 *garniture* ribbons and jewels used as trimmings to a suit
579 *glove* often trimmed with ribbons, gold braid, lace, or fur, and
    scented with jasmine, tuberose, cordivant, orangery, or frangipan
585–6 *red . . . sword* the unofficial uniform of a swaggering officer

D

MANLY

Thy courage will appear more by thy belt than thy sword, I
dare swear.—Then, madam, [*Indicating* PLAUSIBLE] for this
gentle piece of courtesy, this man of tame honour, what
could you find in him? Was it his languishing, affected tone,   590
his mannerly look, his second-hand flattery, the refuse of the
playhouse tiring-rooms? Or his slavish obsequiousness, in
watching at the door of your box at the playhouse for your
hand to your chair? Or his janty way of playing with your
fan? Or was it the gunpowder spot on his hand, or the jewel   595
in his ear, that purchased your heart?

OLIVIA

Good jealous captain, no more of your—

LORD PLAUSIBLE

No, let him go on, madam, for perhaps he may make you
laugh; and I would contribute to your pleasure any way.

MANLY

Gentle rogue!   600

OLIVIA

No, noble captain, you cannot, sure, think anything could
take me more than that heroic title of yours, captain; for
you know we women love honour inordinately.

NOVEL

Ha ha! Faith, she is with thee, bully, for thy raillery.

MANLY *(Aside to* NOVEL)

Faith, so shall I be with you, no bully, for your grinning.   605

OLIVIA

Then, that noble lion-like mien of yours, that soldier-like
weather-beaten complexion, and that manly roughness of
your voice, how can they otherwise than charm us women,
who hate effeminacy!

NOVEL

Ha ha! Faith, I can't hold from laughing.   610

MANLY *(Aside to* NOVEL)

Nor shall I from kicking anon.

592 *tiring-rooms* dressing-rooms
594 *hand to your chair* Plausible escorts Olivia to her sedan after the
     play.
594 *janty* well-bred, genteel, elegant
595 *gunpowder spot* a blue beauty spot tattooed into the skin with gun-
     powder; Wycherley's *Miscellany Poems* (1704) include verses '*Upon
     the* Gun-powder Spot *on a* LADY's Hand'

OLIVIA

And then, that captain-like carelessness in your dress, but especially your scarf; 'twas just such another, only a little higher tied, made me in love with my tailor as he passed by my window the last training day; for we women adore a   615 martial man, and you have nothing wanting to make you more one, or more agreeable, but a wooden leg.

LORD PLAUSIBLE

Nay, i'faith, there your ladyship was a wag; and it was fine, just, and well rallied.

NOVEL

Ay ay, madam, with you ladies too martial men must needs   620 be very killing.

MANLY

Peace, you Bartholomew Fair buffoons!—and be not you vain that these laugh on your side, for they will laugh at their own dull jests. But no more of 'em, for I will only suffer now this lady to be witty and merry.   625

OLIVIA

You would not have your panegyric interrupted. I go on then to your humour. Is there anything more agreeable than the pretty sullenness of that? Than the greatness of your courage, which most of all appears in your spirit of contradiction, for you dare give all mankind the lie; and your   630 opinion is your only mistress, for you renounce that too when it becomes another man's.

NOVEL

Ha ha! I cannot hold; I must laugh at thee, tar, faith!

LORD PLAUSIBLE

And i'faith, dear captain, I beg your pardon and leave to laugh at you too, though I protest I mean you no hurt; but   635 when a lady rallies, a stander-by must be complaisant and do her reason in laughing. Ha ha!

---

613 *scarf* sash worn round the waist or across the chest to indicate military rank; the *London Gazette* no. 2445 (15–18 April 1689) has: 'Lost . . . an Officers Scarf, with four Fringes of Gold round the Wast, set on crimson silk, a very deep fringe at each end'

615 *training day* legally appointed times for drilling the part-time soldiers of a train band; Olivia's insult is doubly galling, since ladies' tailors were traditionally thought effeminate

622 *Bartholomew Fair* the great cloth fair held annually at Smithfield from 24 August to 7 September; in 1668 Pepys saw there puppets, acrobats, rope-dancers, and an educated horse

637 *reason* justice

MANLY

Why, you impudent, pitiful wretches, you presume, sure,
upon your effeminacy to urge me, for you are in all things
so like women that you may think it in me a kind of   640
cowardice to beat you.

OLIVIA

No hectoring, good captain.

MANLY

Or perhaps you think this lady's presence secures you. But
have a care; she has talked herself out of all the respect I
had for her, and by using me ill before you has given me a   645
privilege of using you so before her. But if you would
preserve your respect to her, and not be beaten before her,
go, be gone immediately.

NOVEL

Be gone! What?

LORD PLAUSIBLE

Nay, worthy, noble, generous captain.   650

MANLY

Be gone, I say.

NOVEL

Be gone again! To us, be gone!

MANLY

No chattering, baboons; instantly be gone, or—

(MANLY *puts 'em out of the room;* NOVEL *struts,*
PLAUSIBLE *cringes*)

NOVEL

Well, madam, we'll go make the cards ready in your bedchamber; sure, you will not stay long with him.   655

(*Exeunt* PLAUSIBLE [*and*] NOVEL)

OLIVIA

Turn hither your rage, good Captain Swagger-huff, and be
saucy with your mistress, like a true captain; but be civil to
your rivals and betters, and do not threaten anything but me
here, no, not so much as my windows; nor do not think
yourself in the lodgings of one of your suburb mistresses   660
beyond the Tower.

642 *hectoring* blustering, cf. '*Hector,* a Vaporing, Swaggering Coward'
     (*B.E.*)
647 *your respect to her* your self-respect before her (?)
654–5 *bedchamber* often used for entertaining at this period
657 *saucy* insolent
660–1 *suburb mistresses beyond the Tower* like 2 SAILOR's Blake Kate of
     Wapping (I. 107–8); Otway's *The Poet's Complaint of his Muse*
     (1680) mentions 'a worn-out Suburb-Trull' (327) and 'a *Wapping*
     Drab, or *Shoreditch* Quean' (367)

MANLY

Do not give me cause to think so, for those less infamous
women part with their lovers, just as you did from me, with
unforced vows of constancy and floods of willing tears, but
the same winds bear away their lovers and their vows; and   665
for their grief, if the credulous, unexpected fools return,
they find new comforters, fresh cullies, such as I found here.
The mercenary love of those women too suffers shipwreck
with their gallants' fortunes; now you have heard chance has
used me scurvily, therefore you do too. Well, persevere in   670
your ingratitude, falsehood, and disdain; have constancy in
something, and I promise you to be as just to your real
scorn as I was to your feigned love, and henceforward will
despise, contemn, hate, loathe, and detest you, most faithfully.   675

Enter LETTICE

OLIVIA

Get the ombre cards ready in the next room, Lettice, and—
                    (Whispers to LETTICE *[who then goes out])*

FREEMAN

Bravely resolved, captain.

FIDELIA

And you'll be sure to keep your word, I hope, sir.

MANLY

I hope so too.

FIDELIA

Do you but hope it, sir? If you are not as good as your   680
word, 'twill be the first time you ever bragged, sure.

MANLY

She has restored my reason with my heart.

FREEMAN

But now you talk of restoring, captain, there are other things
which, next to one's heart, one would not part with: I mean
your jewels and money, which it seems she has, sir.   685

MANLY

What's that to you, sir?

668 *suffers* Q2–8, 0 (suffer Q1)

---

675 s.d. *Enter* LETTICE presumably summoned by Olivia during the cli-
    max of Manly's tirade—and what could be more heartless?
676 *ombre* a fashionable game for three players, using only forty cards;
    Lettice must remove the eights, nines, and tens

FREEMAN

Pardon me; whatsoever is yours, I have a share in't, I'm
sure, which I will not lose for asking, though you may be
too generous or too angry now to do't yourself.

FIDELIA

Nay, then I'll make bold to make my claim too.   690

(Both going towards OLIVIA*)*

MANLY

Hold, you impertinent, officious fops! *(Aside)* How have I
been deceived!

FREEMAN

Madam, there are certain appurtenances to a lover's heart,
called jewels, which always go along with it.

FIDELIA

And which, with lovers, have no value in themselves, but   695
from the heart they come with. Our captain's, madam, it
seems you scorn to keep, and much more will those worthless things without it, I am confident.

OLIVIA

A gentleman so well made as you are may be confident; us
easy women could not deny you anything you ask, if 'twere   700
for yourself, but since 'tis for another, I beg your leave to
give him my answer. *(Aside)* An agreeable young fellow,
this, and would not be my aversion! *[Aloud]*—Captain,
your young friend here has a very persuading face, I confess; yet you might have asked me yourself for those trifles   705
you left with me, which—*(Aside to* MANLY*)* hark you a little,
for I dare trust you with the secret; you are a man of so
much honour, I'm sure. I say, then, not expecting your
return, or hoping ever to see you again, I have delivered
your jewels to—   710

MANLY

Whom?

OLIVIA

My husband.

MANLY

Your husband!

OLIVIA

Ay, my husband; for, since you could leave me, I am lately
and privately married to one who is a man of so much   715
honour and experience in the world that I dare not ask him
for your jewels again, to restore 'em to you, lest he should
conclude you never would have parted with 'em to me on
any other score but the exchange of my honour, which

rather than you'd let me lose, you'd lose, I'm sure, yourself   720
those trifles of yours.

MANLY

Triumphant impudence! But married too!

OLIVIA

O, speak not so loud; my servants know it not. I am married; there's no resisting one's destiny or love, you know.

MANLY

Why, did you love him too?   725

OLIVIA

Most passionately; nay, love him now, though I have married him, and he me; which mutual love I hope you are too
good, too generous, a man to disturb by any future claim or
visits to me. 'Tis true, he is now absent in the country, but
returns shortly; therefore I beg of you, for your own ease   730
and quiet and my honour, you will never see me more.

MANLY

I wish I never had seen you.

OLIVIA

But if you should ever have anything to say to me hereafter, let that young gentleman there be your messenger.

MANLY

You would be kinder to him. I find he should be welcome.   735

OLIVIA

Alas, his youth would keep my husband from suspicions and
his visits from scandal; for we women may have pity for
such as he, but no love. And I already think you do not well
to spirit him away to sea, and the sea is already but too rich
with the spoils of the shore.   740

MANLY *(Aside)*

True perfect woman! If I could say anything more injurious
to her now, I would; for I could out-rail a bilked whore or
a kicked coward. But, now I think on't, that were rather to
discover my love than hatred; and I must not talk, for
something I must do.   745

OLIVIA

(Aside) I think I have given him enough of me now, never to
be troubled with him again.

Enter LETTICE

[*Aloud*] Well, Lettice, are the cards and all ready within? I
come then.—Captain, I beg your pardon. You will not make
one at ombre?   750

742 *bilked* cheated

MANLY

No, madam; but I'll wish you a little good luck before you
go.

OLIVIA

No, if you would have me thrive, curse me; for that you'll
do heartily, I suppose.

MANLY

Then, if you will have it so, may all the curses light upon   755
you women ought to fear and you deserve! First, may the
curse of loving play attend your sordid covetousness, and
fortune cheat you by trusting to her as you have cheated
me; the curse of pride, or a good reputation, fall on your
lust; the curse of affectation on your beauty; the curse of   760
your husband's company on your pleasures, and the curse of
your gallant's disappointments in his absence; and the curse
of scorn, jealousy, or despair on your love; and then the
curse of loving on!

OLIVIA

And to requite all your curses, I will only return you your   765
last; may the curse of loving me still fall upon your proud,
hard heart, that could be so cruel to me in these horrid
curses! But heaven forgive you!   (*Exit* OLIVIA)

MANLY

Hell and the devil reward thee!

FREEMAN

Well, you see now mistresses, like friends, are lost by letting 770
'em handle your money; and most women are such kind of
witches, who can have no power over a man unless you give
'em money; but when once they have got any from you,
they never leave you till they have all. Therefore I never dare
give a woman a farthing.   775

MANLY

Well, there is yet this comfort: by losing one's money with
one's mistress, a man is out of danger of getting another, of
being made prize again by love, who, like a pirate, takes you
by spreading false colours, but when once you have run your
ship aground, the treacherous picaroon loofs, so by your   780
ruin you save yourself from slavery at least.

Enter BOY

762 *your gallant's disappointments* i.e., your lover's incapacity to satisfy
    you
779 *spreading false colours* flying unauthorized flags
780 *picaroon* privateer
780 *loofs* luffs, sails near the wind

BOY

Mistress Lettice, here's Madam Blackacre come to wait upon
her honour.   [*Exeunt* LETTICE *and* BOY]

MANLY

D'ye hear that? Let us be gone before she comes; for henceforward I'll avoid the whole damned sex for ever, and   785
woman as a sinking ship.   (*Exeunt* MANLY *and* FIDELIA)

FREEMAN

And I'll stay, to revenge on her your quarrel to the sex, for
out of love to her jointure and hatred to business I would
marry her, to make an end of her thousand suits and my
thousand engagements, to the comfort of two unfortunate   790
sorts of people: my plaintiffs and her defendants, my
creditors and her adversaries.

Enter WIDOW BLACKACRE, *led in by* MAJOR OLDFOX, *and*
JERRY BLACKACRE *following, laden with green bags*

WIDOW

'Tis an arrant sea-ruffian, but I am glad I met with him at
last, to serve him again, major, for the last service was not
good in law.—Boy, duck, Jerry, where is my paper of memo-   795
randums? Give me, child. So. Where is my cousin Olivia
now, my kind relation?

FREEMAN

Here is one that would be your kind relation, madam.

WIDOW

What mean you, sir?

FREEMAN

Why, faith, to be short, to marry you, widow.   800

WIDOW

Is not this the wild, rude person we saw at Captain Manly's?

JERRY

Ay, forsooth, an't please.

WIDOW

What would you? What are you? Marry me!

FREEMAN

Ay, faith, for I am a younger brother and you are a widow.

WIDOW

You are an impertinent person, and go about your business.   805

790 *engagements* legal obligations, here to his creditors
794 *last service* see I. 493
804 *younger brother* i.e., without an inheritance, and so usually reduced
   to the church, the army, or a rich marriage

FREEMAN

I have none, but to marry thee, widow.

WIDOW

But I have other business, I'd have you to know.

FREEMAN

But you have no business a-nights, widow, and I'll make you
pleasanter business than any you have. For a-nights, I assure
you, I am a man of great business; for the business—   810

WIDOW

Go; I'm sure you're an idle fellow.

FREEMAN

Try me but, widow, and employ me as you find my abilities
and industry.

OLDFOX

Pray be civil to the lady, Master—; she's a person of quality,
a person that is no person—   815

FREEMAN

Yes, but she's a person that is a widow. Be you mannerly to
her, because you are to pretend only to be her squire, to
arm her to her lawyer's chambers; but I will be impudent
and bawdy, for she must love and marry me.

WIDOW

Marry come up, you saucy, familiar Jack! You think with   820
us widows 'tis no more than up and ride. Gad forgive me,
nowadays every idle, young, hectoring, roaring companion,
with a pair of turned red breeches and a broad back, thinks
to carry away any widow of the best degree; but I'd have
you to know, sir, all widows are not got, like places at court,   825
by impudence and importunity only.

OLDFOX

No, no, soft, soft; you are a young man and not fit—

FREEMAN

For a widow? Yes, sure, old man, the fitter.

OLDFOX

Go to, go to; if others had not laid in their claims before
you—   830

FREEMAN

Not you, I hope.

812 *Try me but* Only try me
817 *pretend* claim, presume
818 *arm her* walk arm in arm with her
823 *turned* i.e., remade inside out, for economy's sake
824 *carry away* win

OLDFOX

Why not I, sir? Sure, I am a much more proportionable match for her than you, sir; I, who am an elder brother, of a comfortable fortune, and of equal years with her.

WIDOW

How's that? You unmannerly person, I'd have you to know   835
I was born but in *ann' undec' Caroli prim'*.

OLDFOX

Your pardon, lady, your pardon; be not offended with your very servant.—But I say, sir, you are a beggarly younger brother, twenty years younger than her, without any land or stock but your great stock of impudence. Therefore what   840
pretension can you have to her?

FREEMAN

You have made it for me. First, because I am a younger brother.

[OLDFOX]

Why, is that a sufficient plea to a relict? How appears it, sir? By what foolish custom?   845

FREEMAN

By custom time out of mind only. Then, sir, because I have nothing to keep me after her death, I am the likelier to take care of her life. And for my being twenty years younger than her and having a sufficient stock of impudence, I leave it to her whether they will be valid exceptions to me in her   850
widow's law or equity.

OLDFOX

Well, she has been so long in Chancery that I'll stand to her equity and decree between us. *(Aside to the* WIDOW*)* Come, lady, pray snap up this young snap at first, or we shall be troubled with him. Give him a city widow's answer: that is,   855
with all the ill breeding imaginable. Come, madam.

843 s.p. [OLDFOX] ed. (WIDOW Q1–8, 0)

---

836 *ann' undec' Caroli prim'* Law Latin, in the form used for dating statutes, for the eleventh year of Charles I's reign: 1636
838 *very servant* true and professed admirer
851 *law or equity* i.e., whether the widow judges by the strict letter of the law, or by general principles of justice
852 *Chancery* the chief court of equity
852 *stand to* obey, be bound by
853 *decree* the judgment of an equity court
854 *snap up this young snap* speak sharply to this young fellow
854 *at first* at once, immediately

WIDOW

Well then, to make an end of this foolish wooing, for
nothing interrupts business more. First, for you, major

OLDFOX

You declare in my favour then?

FREEMAN

What, direct the court? *(To* JERRY*)* Come, young lawyer,   860
thou shalt be a counsel for me.

JERRY

Gad, I shall betray your cause then, as well as an older
lawyer, never stir.

WIDOW

First, I say, for you, major, my walking hospital of an
ancient foundation, thou bag of mummy, that wouldst fall   865
asunder if 'twere not for thy cerecloths—

OLDFOX

How, lady?

FREEMAN

Ha ha—

JERRY

Hey, brave mother! Use all suitors thus, for my sake.

WIDOW

Thou withered, hobbling, distorted cripple; nay, thou art a   870
cripple all over. Wouldst thou make me the staff of thy age,
the crutch of thy decrepidness? Me—

FREEMAN

Well said, widow! Faith, thou wouldst make a man love
thee now without dissembling.

WIDOW

Thou senseless, impertinent, quibbling, drivelling, feeble,   875
paralytic, impotent, fumbling, frigid nicompoop!

JERRY

Hey, brave mother, for calling of names, i'fac!

WIDOW

Wouldst thou make a caudle-maker, a nurse of me? Can't
you be bed-rid without a bedfellow? Won't your swanskins,

---

863 *never stir* never fear (literally, may I never stir if I don't)
876 *fumbling* cf. '*Fumbler,* an unperforming Husband, one that is in-
      sufficient, a weak Brother' (*B.E.*)
878 *candle* an invalid's drink of spiced wine, sugar, and warm, thin
      gruel
879 *swanskins* fine flannel of extraordinary whiteness

furs, flannels, and the scorched trencher keep you warm   880
there? Would you have me your Scotch warming-pan, with
a pox to you? Me—

OLDFOX

O heavens!

FREEMAN

I told you I should be thought the fitter man, major.

JERRY

Ay, you old fobus, and you would have been my guardian,   885
would you? To have taken care of my estate, that half of't
should never come to me, by letting long leases at peppercorn rents?

WIDOW

If I would have married an old man, 'tis well known I might
have married an earl, nay, what's more, a judge, and been   890
covered the winter nights with the lambskins, which I prefer
to the ermines of nobles. And dost thou think I would wrong
my poor minor there for you?

FREEMAN

Your minor is a chopping minor, God bless him.

(Strokes JERRY *on the head)*

OLDFOX

Your minor may be a major of horse or foot for his big-   895
ness; and it seems you will have the cheating of your minor
to yourself.

WIDOW

Pray sir, bear witness. Cheat my minor! I'll bring my action
of the case for the slander.

FREEMAN

Nay, I would bear false witness for thee now, widow, since   900

---

880 *scorched trencher* heated platter, usually of metal or earthenware,
  used as a warming-pan
881 *Scotch warming-pan* 'a chambermaid who lay in the bed a while to
  warm it for the intending occupant' (*OED*); hence, a wench
885 *fobus* fool (?), swindler (? cf. '*Fob,* a cheat, trick' (*B.E.*))
887–8 *peppercorn rents* nominal rents of a peppercorn a year, demanded
  to make a free land lease good in law
891 *lambskins* used to line the robes of judges, who were known as
  'Lamb-skin-men' (*B.E.*)
894 *chopping* strapping, healthy
898–9 *action of the case* '*Action upon the Case* . . . is a general Action
  given for redress of wrongs done to any Man without force, and
  by Law not especially provided for' (Blount); such wrongs include
  slander

you have done me justice and have thought me the fitter
man for you.

WIDOW

Fair and softly, sir; 'tis my minor's case more than my own.
And I must do him justice now on you.

FREEMAN

How? 905

OLDFOX

So then.

WIDOW

You are first, I warrant, some renegado from the inns of
court and the law, and thou'lt come to suffer for't by the
law: that is, be hanged.

JERRY [*To the* WIDOW]

Not about your neck, forsooth, I hope. 910

FREEMAN

But, madam—

OLDFOX

Hear the court.

WIDOW

Thou art some debauched, drunken, lewd, hectering, gaming
companion, and want'st some widow's old gold to nick upon;
but I thank you, sir, that's for my lawyers. 915

FREEMAN

Faith, we should ne'er quarrel about that, for guineas would
serve my turn. But, widow—

WIDOW

Thou art a foul-mouthed boaster of thy lust, a mere bragga-
docio of thy strength for wine and women, and wilt belie
thyself more than thou dost women, and art every way a 920
base deceiver of women; and would deceive me too, would
you?

FREEMAN

Nay, faith, widow, this is judging without seeing the evidence.

WIDOW

I say you are a worn-out whore-master at five and twenty
both in body and fortune, and cannot be trusted by the 925

905 *How?* an interjection, like the modern 'What?'
907 *renegado* deserter
914 *nick upon* gamble with
916 *guineas* i.e., new gold, first minted in 1663; Pepys found them 'very
convenient, and of easy disposal' (29 October 1666)

common wenches of the town lest you should not pay 'em,
nor by the wives of the town lest you should pay 'em; so
you want women, and would have me your bawd to procure
'em for you.

FREEMAN

Faith, if you had any good acquaintance, widow, 'twould   930
be civilly done of thee, for I am just come from sea.

WIDOW

I mean, you would have me keep you that you might turn
keeper, for poor widows are only used like bawds by you:
you go to church with us but to get other women to lie with.
In fine, you are a cheating, chousing spendthrift, and having   935
sold your own annuity, would waste my jointure.

JERRY

And make havoc of our estate personal, and all our old gilt
plate. I should soon be picking up all our mortgaged apostle
spoons, bowls, and beakers out of most of the ale-houses
betwixt 'Hercules' Pillars' and 'The Boatswain' in Wapping;   940
nay, and you'd be scouring amongst my trees, and make 'em
knock down one another like routed, reeling watchmen at
midnight. Would you so, bully?

FREEMAN

Nay, prithee, widow, hear me.

WIDOW

No, sir. I'd have you to know, thou pitiful, paltry, lath-   945
backed fellow, if I would have married a young man, 'tis
well known I could have had any young heir in Norfolk,

926–7 *pay . . . pay* (1) remunerate (2) satisfy (3) requite with just
    deserts; thus whores think him penniless or impotent, wives potent
    and diseased
933 *keeper* a man who keeps mistresses
935 *chousing* swindling
938 *picking up* buying back(?)
938–9 *apostle spoons* 'Old-fashioned silver spoons, the handles of which
    end in figures of the Apostles. They were the usual present of
    sponsors at baptisms.' (*OED*)
940 *Hercules . . . Wapping* i.e., the entire length of London, from the
    east end at Wapping (where 'The Boatswain' has not been identified)
    to 'Hercules' Pillars' at Hyde Park Corner, then at the westernmost
    edge of the city
941 *scouring* rampaging; the scourers were disorderly gangs who roamed
    London by night, breaking windows, molesting wayfarers, and
    knocking down watchmen. Jerry fears his timber would be felled
    and sold.

nay, the hopefull'st young man this day at the King's Bench
bar; I, that am a relict and executrix of known plentiful
assets and parts, who understand myself and the law. And   950
would you have me under covert-baron again? No, sir, no
covert-baron for me.

FREEMAN

But, dear widow, hear me. I value you only, not your
jointure.

WIDOW

Nay, sir, hold there. I know your love to a widow is covet-   955
ousness of her jointure. And a widow a little stricken in
years with a good jointure is like an old mansion house in a
good purchase: never valued, but take one, take t'other; and
perhaps when you are in possession you'd neglect it, let it
drop to the ground, for want of necessary repairs or expenses 960
upon't.

FREEMAN

No, widow, one would be sure to keep all tight when one is
to forfeit one's lease by dilapidation.

WIDOW

Fie fie, I neglect my business with this foolish discourse of
love.—Jerry, child, let me see the list of the jury. I'm sure   965
my cousin Olivia has some relations amongst 'em. But where
is she?

FREEMAN

Nay, widow, but hear me one word only.

WIDOW

Nay, sir, no more, pray. I will no more harken again to your
foolish love-motions than to offers of arbitration.   970

                          (*Exeunt* WIDOW *and* JERRY)

FREEMAN

Well, I'll follow thee yet; for he that has a pretension at
court, or to a widow, must never give over for a little ill
usage.

OLDFOX

Therefore I'll get her by assiduity, patience, and long suffer-

948 *hopefull'st* most promising
948 *King's Bench* 'the supreme court of common law in the kingdom'
     (*OED*)
950 *parts* possessions
951 *under covert-baron* under the protection of her lord—law-French
     term for a married woman
957–8 *in a good purchase* i.e., as part of an estate bought on favourable
     terms

ings, which you will not undergo; for you idle young fellows   975
leave off love when it comes to be business, and industry
gets more women than love.

FREEMAN

Ay, industry, the fool's and old man's merit; but I'll be
industrious too and make a business on't, and get her by law,
wrangling, and contests, and not by sufferings. And, because   980
you are no dangerous rival, I'll give thee counsel, major.

> If you litigious widow e'er would gain,
> Sigh not to her, but by the law complain;
> To her, as to a bawd, defendant sue
> With statutes, and make justice pimp for you.   985
>
> *(Exeunt)*

Finis actus secundi

Act III, Scene i

Westminster Hall

Enter MANLY *and* FREEMAN, *two* SAILORS *behind*

MANLY

I hate this place, worse than a man that has inherited a
Chancery suit. I wish I were well out on't again.

FREEMAN

Why, you need not be afraid of this place, for a man without money needs no more fear a crowd of lawyers than a
crowd of pickpockets.   5

Westminster Hall begun 1097, rebuilt 1399, and housing from 1224
to 1882 the law courts of England: Common Pleas at the lower
end, and at the upper the King's Bench on the right and Chancery
on the left; Equity and the Exchequer shared an adjacent chamber.
At this period, the hall was lined with stalls selling books, law
stationery, haberdashery, and toys.
s.d. *two* SAILORS Tom and Jack, Manly's attendants from Act I;
Jack is addressed at 490, and another 'of your salt-water sharks'
(447), presumably Tom, robs Jerry off-stage between 405 and 428. No
early editions describe their movements, but all difficulties disappear
if we assume that normally they follow Manly throughout.
2 *Chancery suit* 'of eternal continuance, as thousands have found true
by woeful experience' (Tom Brown, *Amusements,* ed. A. L. Hay-
ward (1927), p. 38)

MANLY

This, the reverend of the law would have thought the palace
or residence of justice; but, if it be, she lives here with the
state of a Turkish emperor, rarely seen; and besieged rather
than defended by her numerous black guard here.

FREEMAN

Methinks 'tis like one of their own halls in Christmas time,   10
whither from all parts fools bring their money to try by the
dice (not the worst judges) whether it shall be their own or
no; but after a tedious fretting and wrangling they drop
away all their money on both sides, and, finding neither the
better at last, go emptily and lovingly away together to the   15
tavern, joining their curses against the young lawyers' box,
that sweeps all like the old ones.

MANLY

Spoken like a revelling Christmas lawyer.

FREEMAN

Yes, I was one, I confess, but was fain to leave the law out
of conscience and fall to making false musters; rather chose   20
to cheat the king than his subjects, plunder rather than take
fees.

MANLY

Well, a plague and a purse-famine light on the law, and that

6 *the reverend . . . thought* either 'those who respect the law would
    suppose' or 'respected lawyers would like us to think'
9 *black guard* a triple pun: (1) the Emperor's swarthy attendants (2)
    black-robed lawyers (3) a gang of street urchins who lived on their
    wits and tongues, like the lawyers: *'We . . . are the* City Black-Guard
    . . . *give us a Penny or a Half-penny amongst us, and you shall
    hear any of us . . . say the* Lords-Prayer *backwards, Swear the* Com-
    pass *round; give a new Curse to every step in the* Monument, *call a*
    Whore *as many proper Names as a* Peer *has Titles'* (Ned Ward, *The
    London Spy,* ed. Ralph Straus (1924), pp. 36–7)
10 *Christmas time* At the Inns of Court, gambling was permitted and
    legal between Christmas and Twelfth Night.
13–14 *drop away* lose
16 *young lawyers' box* i.e., the house 'bank': 'what the Dicers allow
    out of each winning to the Butlers Box, usually amounts to about
    50 *l.* a day and night, wherewith, a small Contribution from each
    Student, are the great charges of the whole *Christmas* defrayed'
    (Chamberlayne, II, 230–1)
17 *the old ones* i.e., the old lawyers' cash-box; in gambling and litiga-
    tion, the contestants both lose, and only the lawyers' boxes gain
20 *false musters* Army officers were paid subsistence for each man on
    their muster-roll; sometimes they entered false names and pocketed
    the cash, like Plume in Farquhar's *The Recruiting Officer* (1706,
    I. i).

female limb of it who dragged me hither today! But prithee,
go see if in that crowd of daggled gowns there *(Pointing to a*   25
crowd of lawyers at the end of the stage), thou canst find her.
                                         (Exit FREEMAN*)*

Manet MANLY

How hard it is to be an hypocrite!
At least to me, who am but newly so.
I thought it once a kind of knavery,
Nay, cowardice, to hide one's faults; but now   30
The common frailty, love, becomes my shame.
He must not know I love th'ungrateful still,
Lest he contemn me more than she; for I,
It seems, can undergo a woman's scorn
But not a man's—   35

Enter to him FIDELIA

FIDELIA
Sir, good sir, generous captain.
MANLY
Prithee, kind impertinence, leave me. Why should'st thou
follow me, flatter my generosity now, since thou know'st I
have no money left? If I had it, I'd give it thee to buy my
quiet.   40
FIDELIA
I never followed yet, sir, reward or fame, but you alone; nor
do I now beg anything but leave to share your miseries. You
should not be a niggard of 'em, since, methinks, you have
enough to spare. Let me follow you now because you hate
me, as you have often said.   45
MANLY
I ever hated a coward's company, I must confess.
FIDELIA
Let me follow you till I am none, then, for you, I'm sure,
will through such worlds of dangers that I shall be inured to
'em; nay, I shall be afraid of your anger more than danger,
and so turn valiant out of fear. Dear captain, do not cast me   50

---

25 *daggled* spattered with mud
25–6 s.d. *(Pointing . . . stage)* probably in the wings, though Raymond
        Williams supposes them painted on the back scene *(Drama in Per-*
        formance (1954, rev. 1968), p. 85)

off till you have tried me once more; do not, do not go to
sea again without me.

MANLY

Thou to sea! To court, thou fool. Remember the advice I
gave thee: thou art a handsome spaniel, and canst fawn
naturally. Go, busk about, and run thyself into the next   55
great man's lobby. First fawn upon the slaves without, and
then run into the lady's bedchamber; thou may'st be admitted
at last to tumble her bed. Go, seek, I say, and lose me, for I
am not able to keep thee. I have not bread for myself.

FIDELIA

Therefore I will not go, because then I may help and serve   60
you.

MANLY

Thou!

FIDELIA

I warrant you, sir; for at worst I could beg or steal for you.

MANLY

Nay, more bragging! Dost thou not know there's venturing
your life in stealing? Go, prithee, away. Thou art as hard to   65
shake off as that flattering, effeminating mischief, love.

FIDELIA

Love, did you name? Why, you are not so miserable as to be
yet in love, sure?

MANLY

No, no; prithee away, be gone, or—. (Aside) I had almost
discovered my love and shame. Well, if I had? That thing   70
could not think the worse of me.—Or if he did?—No.—
Yes, he shall know it—he shall—but then I must never leave
him, for they are such secrets that make parasites and pimps
lords of their masters; for any slavery or tyranny is easier
than love's.—[To FIDELIA] Come hither. Since thou art so   75
forward to serve me, hast thou but resolution enough to
endure the torture of a secret? For such, to some, is in-
supportable.

FIDELIA

I would keep it as safe as if your dear, precious life
depended on't.   80

71 *if he* Q1–2, 0 (if I Q3–8)

55 *busk about* cruise around
64–5 *venturing . . . stealing* Robbery and great larceny, 'when the things
   stollen exceed the value of 12 pence', were felonies punishable by
   death (Phillips).

MANLY

Damn your dearness. It concerns more than my life—my honour.

FIDELIA

Doubt it not, sir.

MANLY

And do not discover it by too much fear of discovering it; but have a great care you let not Freeman find it out.   85

FIDELIA

I warrant you, sir. I am already all joy with the hopes of your commands, and shall be all wings in the execution of 'em; speak quickly, sir.

MANLY

You said you would beg for me.

FIDELIA

I did, sir.   90

MANLY

Then you shall beg for me.

FIDELIA

With all my heart, sir.

MANLY

That is, pimp for me.

FIDELIA

How, sir!

MANLY

D'ye start? Think'st thou, thou could'st do me any other   95
service? Come, no dissembling honour. I know you can do it handsomely; thou wert made for't. You have lost your time with me at sea; you must recover it.

FIDELIA

Do not, sir, beget yourself more reasons for your aversion to me, and make my obedience to you a fault. I am the   100
unfittest in the world to do you such a service.

MANLY

Your cunning arguing against it shows but how fit you are for it. No more dissembling. Here, I say, you must go use it for me to Olivia.

FIDELIA

To her, sir?   105

---

88 *quickly, sir* Q1–2, 0 (quickly Q3–8)

97 *lost* wasted

MANLY

Go flatter, lie, kneel, promise, anything to get her for me. I
cannot live unless I have her. Didst thou not say thou
wouldst do anything to save my life? And she said you had
a persuading face.

FIDELIA

But did not you say, sir, your honour was dearer to you   110
than your life? And would you have me contribute to the
loss of that, and carry love from you to the most infamous,
most false, and—

MANLY *(Sighs, aside)*

And most beautiful!

FIDELIA

—most ungrateful woman that ever lived? For sure she must   115
be so that could desert you so soon, use you so basely, and
so lately too. Do not, do not forget it, sir, and think—

MANLY

No, I will not forget it, but think of revenge. I will lie with
her out of revenge. Go, be gone, and prevail for me, or never
see me more.   120

FIDELIA

You scorned her last night.

MANLY

I know not what I did last night; I dissembled last night.

FIDELIA

Heavens!

MANLY

Be gone, I say, and bring me love or compliance back, or
hopes at least, or I'll never see thy face again, by—   125

FIDELIA

O do not swear, sir; first hear me.

MANLY

I am impatient; away, you'll find me here till twelve.

(Turns away)

FIDELIA

Sir—

MANLY

Not one word, no insinuating argument more, or soothing
persuasion; you'll have need of all your rhetoric with her.   130

---

121 *last night* Eliza's departure for the play in II. 463 suggests that
Manly's interview with Olivia took place during the late afternoon.

Go, strive to alter her, not me; be gone.
(Exit MANLY *at the end of the stage [followed by* SAILORS])

Manet FIDELIA

FIDELIA

Should I discover to him now my sex,
And lay before him his strange cruelty,
'Twould but incense it more.—No, 'tis not time.
For his love must I then betray my own?   135
Were ever love or chance, till now, severe?
Or shifting woman posed with such a task?
Forced to beg that which kills her, if obtained,
And give away her lover not to lose him!   *(Exit* FIDELIA)

Enter WIDOW BLACKACRE *in the middle of half a dozen lawyers,*
whispered to by a fellow in black; JERRY BLACKACRE *following*
the crowd [which includes SERJEANT PLODDON, QUAINT, BLUNDER,
and PETULANT]

WIDOW

Offer me a reference, you saucy companion, you! D'ye know   140
who you speak to? Art thou a solicitor in Chancery, and
offer a reference? A pretty fellow!—Master Serjeant
Ploddon, here's a fellow has the impudence to offer me a
reference.

SERJEANT PLODDON

Who's that has the impudence to offer a reference within   145
these walls?

WIDOW

Nay, for a splitter of causes to do't!

SERJEANT PLODDON

No, madam; to a lady learned in the law, as you are, the
offer of a reference were to impose upon you.

WIDOW

No no, never fear me for a reference, Master Serjeant. But   150
come, have you not forgot your brief? Are you sure you
shan't make the mistake of—hark you. *(Whispers)* Go, then,

---

137 *shifting* evasive, deceitful
140 *reference* i.e., to settle out of court by submitting a controversial
    Chancery suit to the Master in Ordinary for arbitration, which
    would rob the Widow of her fun
147 *splitter of causes* lawyer who subdivided a suit, pleaded each part
    separately and so earned multiple fees; the Widow retains a Master
    Splitcause in her Chancery suit at 272

go to your Court of Common Pleas, and say one thing
over and over again. You do it so naturally you'll never be
suspected for protracting time.   155

SERJEANT PLODDON

Come, I know the course of the court, and your business.

(Exit SERJEANT PLODDON*)*

WIDOW

Let's see, Jerry, where are my minutes?—Come, Master
Quaint, pray go talk a great deal for me in Chancery; let
your words be easy and your sense hard; my cause requires
it. Branch it bravely, and deck my cause with flowers that the   160
snake may lie hidden. Go, go, and be sure you remember the
decree of my Lord Chancellor *tricesimo quart'* of the Queen.

QUAINT

I will, as I see cause, extenuate or examplify matter of fact,
baffle truth with impudence, answer exceptions with questions, though never so impertinent; for reasons give 'em   165
words, for law and equity tropes and figures; and so relax
and enervate the sinews of their argument with the oil of my
eloquence. But when my lungs can reason no longer, and
not being able to say anything more for our cause, say everything of our adversary, whose reputation, though never so   170
clear and evident in the eye of the world, yet with sharp
invectives—

WIDOW

Alias, Billingsgate.

---

163 *examplify* Q1, 0 (amplify Q2–8)

---

153 *Common Pleas* 'so called, because there are debated the usual
   Pleas between Subject and Subject . . . None but Sergeants at Law
   may plead in this Court' (Chamberlayne, II, 100)
158 *Chancery* 'the Court of Equity & Conscience, moderating the
   severity of other Courts that are more strictly tied to the rigour of
   the Law' (Phillips); 'the less it is perplexed with the quirks of
   Lawyers the more it is guided by Conscience' (Chamberlayne,
   II, 120–1)
160 *Branch it bravely* Decorate it handsomely (with rhetorical ornament)
162 *tricesimo . . . Queen* the thirty-fourth year of Elizabeth I's reign:
   1591
163 *extenuate or examplify* diminish or enlarge
163 *matter of fact* legal term used to distinguish verifiable fact from
   inference or opinion
164 *baffle* confuse, deceive
165 *impertinent* irrelevant or trivial
173 *Billingsgate* 'Scolding, ill Language, foul Words' (*B.E.*), common at
   the fish market in Thames Street

QUAINT

—with poignant and sour invectives, I say, I will deface, wipe out, and obliterate his fair reputation, even as a record   175
with the juice of lemons; and tell such a story (for the truth on't is, all that we can do for our client in Chancery is telling a story), a fine story, a long story, such a story—

WIDOW

Go, save thy breath for the cause; talk at the bar, Master Quaint. You are so copiously fluent you can weary anyone's   180
ears sooner than your own tongue. Go, weary our adversary's counsel and the court. Go, thou art a fine-spoken person. Adad, I shall make thy wife jealous of me, if you can but court the court into a decree for us. Go, get you gone, and remember—*(Whispers)*   *(Exit* QUAINT*)*   185
Come, Master Blunder, pray bawl soundly for me at the King's Bench. Bluster, sputter, question, cavil; but be sure your argument be intricate enough to confound the court, and then you do my business. Talk what you will, but be sure your tongue never stand still, for your own noise will   190
secure your sense from censure. 'Tis like coughing or hemming when one has got the belly-ache, which stifles the unmannerly noise. Go, dear rogue, and succeed; and I'll invite thee ere it be long to more soused venison.

BLUNDER

I'll warrant you, after your verdict your judgment shall not   195
be arrested upon if's and and's.   [*Exit* BLUNDER]

WIDOW

Come, Master Petulant, let me give you some new instructions for our cause in the Exchequer. Are the Barons sat?

PETULANT

Yes, no; may be they are, may be they are not. What know I? What care I?   200

184 *gone, and* Q1, 0 (gone, Q2–8)

---

174 *poignant* sharp, severe
183 *Adad* 'an expletive of asseveration or emphasis' *(OED)*
194 *soused* pickled
196 *arrested* i.e., brought to a halt on grounds of error; all proceedings are then set aside and an acquittal given
198 *Exchequer* 'Here are tryed all Causes which belong to the Kings Treasury or Revenue, as touching Accounts, Disbursements, Customs, and all Fines imposed upon any Man' (Chamberlayne, II, 106)
198 *Barons* judges of the Court of Exchequer, 'and they are called *Barons,* because *Barons* of the Realm were wont to be employed in that Office' (Blount)

WIDOW

Heyday! I wish you would but snap up the counsel on
t'other side anon at the bar as much, and have a little more
patience with me, that I might instruct you a little better.

PETULANT

You instruct me! What is my brief for, mistress?

WIDOW

Ay, but you seldom read your brief but at the bar, if you do   205
it then.

PETULANT

Perhaps I do, perhaps I don't, and perhaps 'tis time
enough. Pray hold yourself contented, mistress.

WIDOW

Nay, if you go there too, I will not be contented, sir. Though
you, I see, will lose my cause for want of speaking, I won't.   210
You shall hear me, and shall be instructed. Let's see your
brief.

PETULANT

Send your solicitor to me. Instructed by a woman! I'd
have you to know, I do not wear a bar-gown—

WIDOW

By a woman! And I'd have you to know I am no common   215
woman, but a woman conversant in the laws of the land as
well as yourself, though I have no bar-gown.

PETULANT

Go to, go to, mistress. You are impertinent, and there's your
brief for you. Instruct me!   *(Flings her breviate at her)*

WIDOW

Impertinent to me, you saucy Jack, you! You return my   220
breviate, but where's my fee? You'll be sure to keep that,
and scan that so well that if there chance to be but a brass
half-crown in't, one's sure to hear on't again. Would you
would but look on your breviate half so narrowly! But pray
give me my fee too, as well as my brief.   225

PETULANT

Mistress, that's without precedent. When did a counsel ever
return his fee, pray? And you are impertinent and ignorant
to demand it.

209 *go there* come to that
213 *solicitor* Barristers take their instructions from a client's solicitors,
  not from a client direct.
219 s.d. *breviate* lawyer's brief
222–3 *brass half-crown* a counterfeit; half-crowns were silver

WIDOW

Impertinent again and ignorant, to me! Gadsbodikins, you
puny upstart in the law, to use me so! you green bag carrier,   230
you murderer of unfortunate causes; the clerk's ink is scarce
off of your fingers, you that newly come from lamp-blacking
the judge's shoes and are not fit to wipe mine; you call me
impertinent and ignorant! I would give thee a cuff on the
ear, sitting the courts, if I were ignorant. Marry gep, if it   235
had not been for me, thou hadst been yet but a hearing
counsel at the bar.   *(Exit* PETULANT*)*

Enter MASTER BUTTONGOWN, *crossing the stage in haste*

Master Buttongown, Master Buttongown, whither so fast?
What, won't you stay till we are heard?
BUTTONGOWN

I cannot, Mistress Blackacre, I must be at the council; my   240
lord's cause stays there for me.
WIDOW

And mine suffers here.
BUTTONGOWN

I cannot help it.
WIDOW

I'm undone.
BUTTONGOWN

What's that to me?   245
WIDOW

Consider the five pound fee, if not my cause. That was something to you.
BUTTONGOWN

Away, away; pray be not so troublesome, mistress; I must
be gone.
WIDOW

Nay, but consider a little: I am your old client, my lord but   250
a new one; or let him be what he will, he will hardly be a
better client to you than myself. I hope you believe I shall be

229 *Gadsbodikins* (By) God's (=Christ's) dear body
230 *green bag carrier* see I. 424 note
235 *sitting the courts* The punishment 'For striking in *Westminster-Hall*
    whilst the Courts of Justice are sitting, is imprisonment during life,
    and forfeiture of all [the offender's] Estate' (Chamberlayne, I, 46).
235 *Marry gep* (=By Mary Gipcy=By St Mary of Egypt) 'An exclama-
    tion of asseveration, surprise, indignation, etc.' (*OED*)
236-7 *hearing counsel* barrister without a brief, who attends the courts
    but remains silent

in law as long as I live; therefore am no despicable client.
Well, but go to your lord; I know you expect he should make
you a judge one day, but I hope his promise to you will   255
prove a true lord's promise. But, that he might be sure to
fail you, I wish you had his bond for't.

BUTTONGOWN

But what? Will you yet be thus impertinent, mistress?

[Going]

WIDOW

Nay, I beseech you, sir, stay, if it be but to tell me my lord's
case. Come, in short.   260

BUTTONGOWN

Nay then—   *(Exit* BUTTONGOWN*)*

WIDOW

Well, Jerry, observe, child, and lay it up for hereafter: these
are those lawyers who by being in all causes are in none;
therefore, if you would have 'em for you, let your adversary
see 'em, for he may chance to depend upon 'em, and so in   265
being against thee they'll be for thee.

JERRY

Ay, mother; they put me in mind of the unconscionable
wooers of widows, who undertake briskly their matrimonial
business for their money, but when they have got it once,
let who s' will drudge for them. Therefore have a care of   270
'em, forsooth. There's advice for your advice.

WIDOW

Well said, boy.—Come, Master Splitcause, pray go see
when my cause in Chancery comes on, and go speak with
Master Quillet in the King's Bench and Master Quirk in the
Common Pleas, and see how our matters go there.   275

Enter MAJOR OLDFOX

OLDFOX

Lady, a good and propitious morning to you, and may all
your causes go as well as if I myself were judge of 'em.

WIDOW

Sir, excuse me; I am busy, and cannot answer compliments

268–9 *matrimonial business* sexual intercourse
274 *Quillet . . . Quirk* type names for a verbal subtlety or evasion
274 *King's Bench* 'where the King was wont to sit in his own person'
(Phillips); 'in this Court are handled the Pleas of the Crown, all
things that concern loss of life, or Member of any Subject . . . all
Treasons, Felonies, breach of Peace, Oppression, Mis-government'
(Chamberlayne, II, 96)

in Westminster Hall.—Go, Master Splitcause, and come to
me again to that bookseller's; there I'll stay for you, that you   280
may be sure to find me.

OLDFOX

No, sir, come to the other bookseller's.—I'll attend your
ladyship thither.   (*Exit* SPLITCAUSE)

WIDOW

Why to the other?

OLDFOX

Because he is my bookseller, lady.   285

WIDOW

What, to sell you lozenges for your catarrh or medicines for
your corns? What else can a major deal with a bookseller
for?

OLDFOX

Lady, he prints for me.

WIDOW

Why, are you an author?   290

OLDFOX

Of some few essays; deign you, lady, to peruse 'em. (*Aside*)
She is a woman of parts, and I must win her by showing
mine.

The BOOKSELLER'*s* BOY [*comes forward*]

BOY

Will you see Culpeper, mistress? *Aristotle's Problems? The
Complete Midwife?*   295

WIDOW

No; let's see Dalton, Hughes, Sheppard, Wingate.

BOY

We have no law books.

294–5 *Culpeper . . . Midwife* popular medical guides: Nicholas Culpeper's famous herbal, *The English Physitian* (1652), reached seven
   editions by 1669, the spurious *Problemes of Aristotle with other
   Philosophers and Phisitions* (1595) was reprinted in 1670, and T.C.'s
   The Compleat Midwifes Practice (1656) reached a third edition in
   1663; as the Boy is not precise in his offer, other titles may be
   intended
296 *Dalton . . . Wingate* legal authors: the seventh edition of Michael
   Dalton's *The Countrey Iustice* (1618) appeared in 1666; William
   Hughes's most recent book was *Quæries, or choice cases for moots*
   (1675), and William Sheppard's *A Grand Abridgment of the Common and Statute Law* (1675); Edmund Wingate's *The Exact Constable* (?1660) reached its fourth edition in 1676; again, other
   titles by these prolific authors may be intended

WIDOW

No? You are a pretty bookseller, then.

OLDFOX

Come, have you e'er a one of my essays left?

BOY

Yes, sir; we have enough, and shall always have 'em.   300

OLDFOX

How so?

BOY

Why, they are good, steady, lasting ware.

OLDFOX

Nay, I hope they will live; let's see.—Be pleased, madam, to peruse the poor endeavours of my pen; for I have a pen, though I say it, that—   *(Gives her a book)*   305

JERRY

Pray let me see *St George for Christendom*, or *The Seven Champions of England*.

WIDOW

No no; give him *The Young Clerk's Guide.*—What, we shall have you read yourself into a humour of rambling, and fighting, and studying military discipline and wearing red   310 breeches!

OLDFOX

Nay, if you talk of military discipline, show him my *Treatise of the Art Military*.

WIDOW

Hold; I would as willingly he should read a play.

JERRY

O pray, forsooth, mother, let me have a play.   315

WIDOW

No, sirrah; there are young students of the law enough spoiled already by plays. They would make you in love with your laundress, or, what's worse, some queen of the stage

304 *for I have a pen,* Q1, 0 (*omitted* Q2–8)

306–7 *St George . . . England* Amusingly, Jerry confuses the popular old ballad *St George for England* (which Monsieur recommends as whore's reading in Act V of *The Gentleman Dancing-Master*) with Richard Johnson's evergreen prose romance *The most famous History of the Seauen Champions of Christendome* (1596), which reached its seventh edition in 1670.
308 *The Young Clerk's Guide* by Sir Richard Hutton (1650); the fourteenth edition appeared in 1673
310–11 *red breeches* see II. 585–6 note

that was a laundress, and so turn keeper before you are of
age.   320

Several crossing the stage

But stay, Jerry, is not that Master What-d'ye-call-him that
goes there, he that offered to sell me a suit in Chancery for
five hundred pound, for a hundred down and only paying the
clerk's fees?

JERRY

Ay, forsooth; 'tis he.   325

WIDOW

Then stay here, and have a care of the bags whilst I follow
him. Have a care of the bags, I say.

JERRY

And do you have a care, forsooth, of the statute against
champerty, I say.   *(Exit* WIDOW*)*

Enter FREEMAN *to them*

FREEMAN

(Aside) So, there's a limb of my widow, which was wont to   330
be inseparable from her; she can't be far. [*Aloud*] How now,
my pretty son-in-law that shall be, where's my widow?

JERRY

My mother, but not your widow, will be forthcoming
presently.

FREEMAN

Your servant, major. What, are you buying furniture for a   335
little sleeping closet, which you miscall a study? For you do
only by your books as by your wenches: bind 'em up neatly
and make 'em fine, for other people to use 'em; and your
bookseller is properly your upholster, for he furnishes your
room rather than your head.   340

OLDFOX

Well, well, good sea-lieutenant, study you your compass;
that's more than your head can deal with. *(Aside)* I will go
find out the widow, to keep her out of his sight, or he'll
board her whilst I am treating a peace.   *(Exit* OLDFOX*)*

Manent FREEMAN, JERRY[, BOY]

319 *keeper* one who keeps a mistress
329 *champerty* legal term for an illegal bargain where an outsider con-
      tributed to the costs of a suit in exchange for a share of the spoils
      if it succeeded
335 *furniture* furnishings, ornaments, like Olivia's china in II. 446
339 *upholster* a dealer in small items of furniture (the modern *up-
      holsterer* is more limited in application)
344 *treating* negotiating, arranging terms for

E

JERRY [*To* BOY]

Nay, prithee, friend, now let me have but *The Seven Champions*; you shall trust me no longer than till my mother's Master Splitcause comes, for I hope he'll lend me wherewithal to pay for't.

FREEMAN

Lend thee! Here, I'll pay him. Do you want money, squire? I'm sorry a man of your estate should want money. 350

JERRY

Nay, my mother will ne'er let me be at age; and till then, she says—

FREEMAN

At age! Why, you are at age already to have spent an estate, man; there are younger than you have kept their women these three years, have had half a dozen claps, and lost as 355 many thousand pounds at play.

JERRY

Ay, they are happy sparks! Nay, I know some of my schoolfellows who, when we were at school, were two years younger than me, but now, I know not how, are grown men before me, and go where they will and look to themselves; but my 360 curmudgeonly mother won't allow me wherewithal to be a man of myself with.

FREEMAN

Why, there 'tis; I knew your mother was in the fault. Ask but your schoolfellows what they did to be men of themselves. 365

JERRY

Why, I know they went to law with their mothers, for they say there's no good to be done upon a widow mother till one goes to law with her; but mine is as plaguey a lawyer as any's of our Inn. Then would she marry too, and cut down my trees. Now I should hate, man, to have my father's wife 370 kissed and slapped and t'other thing too (you know what I mean) by another man; and our trees are the purest, tall, even, shady twigs, by my fa—

355 *these* Q1, 0 (this Q2–8)

---

355 *claps* attacks of gonorrhœa
360 *look to* take care of
361–2 *a man of myself* my own master
366 *went to law with* sought legal redress from
372 *purest* finest (an adjective popular with the unsophisticated, like Margery in *The Country Wife* (1675, III. i, 10))

FREEMAN

Come, squire, let your mother and your trees fall as she
pleases, rather than wear this gown and carry green bags all   375
thy life and be pointed at for a Tony. But you shall be able
to deal with her yet the common way: thou shalt make false
love to some lawyer's daughter, whose father, upon the
hopes of thy marrying her, shall lend thee money and law to
preserve thy estate and trees; and thy mother is so ugly   380
nobody will have her, if she cannot cut down thy trees.

JERRY

Nay, if I had but anybody to stand by me, I am as stomachful as another.

FREEMAN

That will I; I'll not see any hopeful young gentleman abused.

BOY *(Aside)*

By any but yourself.   385

JERRY

The truth on't is, mine's as arrant a widow mother to her
poor child as any's in England. She won't so much as let one
have sixpence in one's pocket to see a motion, or the dancing
of the ropes, or—

FREEMAN

Come, you shan't want money; there's gold for you.   390

JERRY

O Lord, sir, two guineas! D'ye lend me this? Is there no trick
in't? Well, sir, I'll give you my bond for security.

FREEMAN

No no, thou hast given me thy face for security; anybody
would swear thou dost not look like a cheat. You shall have
what you will of me, and if your mother will not be kinder   395
to you, come to me, who will.

JERRY

(Aside) By my fa— he's a curious fine gentleman! [*Aloud*]
But will you stand by one?

FREEMAN

If you can be resolute.

JERRY

Can be resolved! Gad, if she gives me but a cross word, I'll   400
leave her tonight and come to you. But now I have got

376 *Tony* 'a silly Fellow, or Ninny' (*B.E.*)
382–3 *stomachful* courageous
388–9 *motion . . . ropes* puppet shows and tightrope walkers, both
    popular entertainments at Bartholomew Fair (see II. 622 note)

money, I'll go to Jack of All Trades at t'other end of the
Hall, and buy the neatest, purest things—

FREEMAN [*Aside*]

And I'll follow the great boy, and my blow at his mother:
steal away the calf, and the cow will follow you.   405

(*Exit* JERRY, *followed by* FREEMAN[; *the* BOOKSELLER'S BOY
retires])

Enter, on the other side, MANLY [*followed by* SECOND SAILOR],
WIDOW BLACKACRE, *and* OLDFOX

MANLY

Damn your cause! Can't you lose it without me?—which
you are like enough to do, if it be, as you say, an honest
one. I will suffer no longer for't.

WIDOW

Nay, captain, I tell you, you are my prime witness; and the
cause is just now coming on, Master Splitcause tells me.   410
Lord, methinks you should take a pleasure in walking here,
as half you see now do, for they have no business here, I
assure you.

MANLY

Yes, but I'll assure you, then, their business is to persecute
me. But d'ye think I'll stay any longer, to have a rogue,   415
because he knows my name, pluck me aside and whisper a
news-book secret to me with a stinking breath? A second
come piping angry from the court, and sputter in my face
his tedious complaints against it? A third law-coxcomb,
because he saw me once at a reader's dinner, come and put   420
me a long law case, to make a discovery of his indefatigable
dullness and my wearied patience? A fourth, a most barbarous civil rogue, who will keep a man half an hour in the
crowd with a bowed body and a hat off, acting the reformed
sign of the Salutation Tavern, to hear his bountiful profes-   425

402 *Jack of All Trades* apparently the name of a stall selling toys
404 *blow at* plot against (?)
417 *news-book secret* A secret that's published is no secret at all.
420 *reader's dinner* banquet given by a distinguished lecturer in law at
one of the Inns of Court: 'During the Readings, which heretofore
was three Weeks and three Days . . . the Reader keeps a Constant
and Sumptuous Feasting, Inviting the Chief Nobles, Judges, Bishops,
Great Officers of the Kingdom, and sometimes the King himself'
(Thomas Delaune, *Angliæ Metropolis* (1690), p. 170)
425 *Salutation Tavern* Pepys visited a tavern of this name in Billingsgate
on 5 March, 1659/60, but there were several others; the sign, reformed under the Commonwealth, showed two men bowing politely,
instead of the Angel Gabriel saluting Mary.

sions of service and friendship, whilst he cares not if I were
damned and I am wishing him hanged out of my way? I'd
as soon run the gauntlet as walk t'other turn.

Enter to them JERRY BLACKACRE *without his bags, but laden with
trinkets, which he endeavours to hide from his mother, and
followed at a distance by* FREEMAN

WIDOW

O, are you come, sir? But where have you been, you ass?
And how come you thus laden?   430

JERRY

Look here, forsooth, mother; now here's a duck, here's a
boar-cat, and here's an owl. *(Making a noise with catcalls,
and other suchlike instruments)*

WIDOW

Yes, there is an owl, sir.

OLDFOX

He's an ungracious bird, indeed.

WIDOW

But go, thou trangam, and carry back those trangams, which 435
thou hast stolen or purloined; for nobody would trust a
minor in Westminster Hall, sure.

JERRY

Hold yourself contented, forsooth; I have these commodities
by a fair bargain and sale, and there stands my witness and
creditor.   440

WIDOW

How's that!—What, sir, d'ye think to get the mother by
giving the child a rattle?—But where are my bags, my writings, you rascal?

JERRY *(Aside)*

O law! Where are they indeed?

WIDOW

How, sirrah? Speak, come—   445

MANLY *(Apart to him)*

You can tell her, Freeman, I suppose?

FREEMAN *(Apart to him)*

'Tis true, I made one of your salt-water sharks steal 'em

---

428 s.d. *trinkets* cheap toys
432 *boar-cat* tom-cat
432 s.d. *catcalls* whistles or squeakers which make funny noises
435 *trangam* (1) pseudo-legal term for anything contemptible (2) toy

whilst he was eagerly choosing his commodities, as he calls
'em, in order to my design upon his mother.

WIDOW

Won't you speak? Where were you, I say, you son of a—an   450
unfortunate woman?—O, major, I'm undone. They are all
that concern my estate, my jointure, my husband's deed of
gift, my evidences for all my suits now depending! What will
become of them?

FREEMAN

(Aside) I'm glad to hear this. [Aloud] They'll be safe, I   455
warrant you, madam.

WIDOW

O where, where? Come, you villain, along with me, and show
me where.   (Exeunt WIDOW, JERRY, OLDFOX)

Manent MANLY, FREEMAN [, SAILOR]

MANLY

Thou hast taken the right way to get a widow, by making
her great boy rebel; for when nothing will make a widow   460
marry, she'll do't to cross her children. But canst thou in
earnest marry this harpy, this volume of shrivelled blurred
parchments and law, this attorney's desk?

FREEMAN

Ay ay, I'll marry and live honestly—that is, give my creditors,
not her, due benevolence: pay my debts.   465

MANLY

Thy creditors, you see, are not so barbarous as to put thee
in prison, and wilt thou commit thyself to a noisome dun-
geon for thy life, which is the only satisfaction thou canst
give thy creditors by this match?

FREEMAN

Why, is not she rich?   470

MANLY

Ay, but he that marries a widow for her money will find
himself as much mistaken as the widow that marries a young
fellow for due benevolence, as you call it.

FREEMAN

Why, d'ye think I shan't deserve wages? I'll drudge faithfully.   475

MANLY

I tell thee again, he that is the slave in the mine has the least
propriety in the ore. You may dig and dig, but if thou

449 *in order to* for the sake of, to bring about

wouldst have her money, rather get to be her trustee than
her husband; for a true widow will make over her estate to
anybody, and cheat herself, rather than be cheated by her   480
children or a second husband.

Enter to them JERRY, *running in a fright*

JERRY

O law! I'm undone, I'm undone! My mother will kill me.—
You said you'd stand by one.

FREEMAN

So I will, my brave squire, I warrant thee.

JERRY

Ay, but I dare not stay till she comes; for she's as furious,   485
now she has lost her writings, as a bitch when she has lost
her puppies.

MANLY

The comparison's handsome!

JERRY

O, she's here!

Enter WIDOW BLACKACRE *and* OLDFOX

FREEMAN *(To the* SAILOR*)*

Take him, Jack, and make haste with him to your master's   490
lodging; and be sure you keep him up till I come.
                                        (Exeunt JERRY *and* SAILOR*)*

WIDOW

O my dear writings! Where's this heathen rogue, my minor?

FREEMAN

Gone to drown or hang himself.

WIDOW

No, I know him too well; he'll ne'er be *felo de se* that way,
but he may go and choose a guardian of his own head and   495
so be *felo de ses biens*, for he has not yet chosen one.

---

491 *up* upstairs (and so out of sight from pursuers in the street)
494 *felo de se* 'Is he that commits Felony by murdring himself'
  (Blount); he is denied Christian burial, and forfeits his goods to the
  Crown
495 *choose a guardian* 'A Son at the age of 14, may chuse his Guardian,
  may claim his Land, . . . may consent to Marriage, may, by Will,
  dispose of Goods and Chattels' (Chamberlayne, I, 297).
495 *of his own head* as he pleases, of his own choice
496 *felo de ses biens* literally 'a felon with regard to his goods': a
  pseudo-legal term coined by the Widow, who fears Jerry will
  appoint a guardian who will mismanage the goods entrusted to him

FREEMAN *(Aside)*

Say you so? And he shan't want one.

WIDOW

But now I think on't, 'tis you, sir, have put this cheat upon
me; for there is a saying, 'take hold of a maid by her smock
and a widow by her writings, and they cannot get from you'.   500
But I'll play fast and loose with you yet, if there be law; and
my minor and writings are not forthcoming, I'll bring my
action of detinue or trover. But first, I'll try to find out this
guardianless, graceless villain. Will you jog, major?

MANLY

If you have lost your evidence, I hope your causes cannot   505
go on, and I may be gone?

WIDOW

O no, stay but a making-water while, as one may say, and
I'll be with you again.   *(Exeunt* WIDOW *and* OLDFOX)

Manent MANLY, FREEMAN

FREEMAN

Well, sure, I am the first man that ever began a love intrigue
in Westminster Hall.   510

MANLY

No, sure; for the love to a widow generally begins here, and
as the widow's cause goes against the heir or executors, the
jointure rivals commence their suit to the widow.

FREEMAN

Well, but how, pray, have you passed your time here since
I was forced to leave you alone? You have had a great deal   515
of patience.

MANLY

Is this a place to be alone or have patience in? But I have
had patience indeed, for I have drawn upon me, since I came,
but three quarrels and two lawsuits.

497 *want* lack
499 *a saying* not known
501–2 *and my* if my
503 *detinue* 'a Writ that lieth against him who having goods or chattels
    delivered him to keep, refuseth to deliver them again' (Phillips)
503 *trover* 'an action against him who having found another mans goods,
    refuseth to deliver them upon demand' (Phillips); the Widow sus-
    pects Jerry of collusion (*detinue*) or negligence (*trover*), but as
    Freeman stole the bags, neither action is appropriate here
507 *a making-water while* so Shadwell's boorish country gentleman has
    'not so much as a pissing while' in Act IV of *The Sullen Lovers*
    (1668)

FREEMAN

Nay, faith, you are too curst to be let loose in the world;   520
you should be tied up again in your sea-kennel, called a ship.
But how could you quarrel here?

MANLY

How could I refrain? A lawyer talked peremptorily and
saucily to me, and as good as gave me the lie.

FREEMAN

They do it so often to one another at the bar, that they make   525
no bones on't elsewhere.

MANLY

However, I gave him a cuff on the ear; whereupon he jogs
two men whose backs were turned to us, for they were reading at a bookseller's, to witness I struck him, sitting the
courts; which office they so readily promised that I called   530
'em rascals and knights of the post. One of 'em presently
calls two other absent witnesses, who were coming towards
us at a distance; whilst the other, with a whisper, desires to
know my name, that he might have satisfaction by way of
challenge as t'other by way of writ, but if it were not rather   535
to direct his brother's writ than his own challenge. There,
you see, is one of my quarrels and two of my lawsuits.

FREEMAN

So; and the other two?

MANLY

For advising a poet to leave off writing and turn lawyer,
because he is dull and impudent, and says or writes nothing   540
now but by precedent.

FREEMAN

And the third quarrel?

MANLY

For giving more sincere advice to a handsome, well-dressed
young fellow, who asked it too, not to marry a wench that
he loved and I had lain with.   545

FREEMAN

Nay, if you will be giving your sincere advice to lovers and
poets, you will not fail of quarrels.

520 *curst* cantankerous, quarrelsome
531 *knights of the post* see 'The Persons', p. 12
531 *presently* immediately
535 *if it were not* i.e., it was surely
547 *fail* keep clear

MANLY

Or if I stay in this place, for I see more quarrels crowding
upon me. Let's be gone and avoid 'em.

Enter NOVEL *at a distance, coming towards them*

A plague on him, that sneer is ominous to us. He is coming   550
upon us, and we shall not be rid of him.

NOVEL

Dear bully, don't look so grum upon me; you told me just
now you had forgiven me a little harmless raillery upon
wooden legs last night.

MANLY

Yes yes; pray be gone, I am talking of business.   555

NOVEL

Can't I hear it? I love thee and will be faithful, and always—

MANLY

Impertinent! 'Tis business that concerns Freeman only.

NOVEL

Well, I love Freeman too, and would not divulge his secret.
Prithee speak, prithee, I must—

MANLY

Prithee let me be rid of thee; I must be rid of thee.   560

NOVEL

Faith, thou canst hardly, I love thee so. Come, I must know
the business.

MANLY

(Aside) So, I have it now. [*Aloud*] Why, if you needs will
know it, he has a quarrel and his adversary bids him bring
two friends with him; now I am one, and we are thinking   565
who we shall have for a third.

Several crossing the stage

NOVEL

A pox, there goes a fellow owes me an hundred pound, and
goes out of town tomorrow. I'll speak with him, and come
to you presently.   *(Exit* NOVEL*)*

MANLY

No, but you won't.   570

FREEMAN

You are dextrously rid of him.

Enter OLDFOX

552 *grum* morose, surly (adj.)
554 *last night* see 121 note

MANLY

To what purpose, since here comes another as impertinent?
I know by his grin he is bound hither.

OLDFOX

Your servant, worthy, noble captain. Well, I have left the
widow, because she carried me from your company; for,   575
faith, captain, I must needs tell thee, thou art the only officer
in England, who was not an Edgehill officer, that I care for.

MANLY

I'm sorry for't.

OLDFOX

Why, wouldst thou have me love them?

MANLY

Anybody, rather than me.   580

OLDFOX

What, you are modest, I see; therefore, too, I love thee.

MANLY

No, I am not modest, but love to brag myself and can't
patiently hear you fight over the last civil war. Therefore, go
look out the fellow I saw just now here, that walks with his
stockings and his sword out at heels, and let him tell you the   585
history of that scar on his cheek, to give you occasion to
show yours, got in the field at Bloomsbury, not that of Edgehill. Go to him, poor fellow; he is fasting and has not yet
the happiness this morning to stink of brandy and tobacco.
Go, give him some to hear you; I am busy.   590

OLDFOX

Well, egad, I love thee now, boy, for thy surliness; thou art
no tame captain, I see, that will suffer—

MANLY

An old fox.

OLDFOX

All that shan't make me angry; I consider thou art peevish,
and fretting at some ill success at law. Prithee, tell me what   595
ill luck you have met with here.

---

586 *scar on his cheek* 'Scars in the face commonly give a man a certain
fierce and martial air, which sets him off to advantage' (Anthony
Hamilton, *Memoirs of the Count de Grammont* (1926), p. 165).

587 *Bloomsbury* The open fields to the north of Southampton House,
where Russell Square now stands, were favourite duelling grounds.

587–8 *Edgehill* in Warwickshire, site of the first major battle of the
Civil War, 23 October 1642; to judge from 616, Oldfox fought on
Cromwell's side

595 *ill success* unfavourable outcome

MANLY

You.

OLDFOX

Do I look like the picture of ill luck? Gadsnouns, I love
thee more and more; and shall I tell thee what made me love
thee first?   600

MANLY

Do; that I may be rid of that damned quality and thee.

OLDFOX

'Twas thy wearing that broadsword there.

MANLY

Here, Freeman, let's change. I'll never wear it more.

OLDFOX

How! You won't, sure. Prithee, don't look like one of our
holiday captains nowadays, with a bodkin by your side, your   605
martinet rogues.

MANLY

(Aside) O, then there's hopes. [*Aloud*] What, d'ye find fault
with martinet? Let me tell you, sir, 'tis the best exercise in
the world, the most ready, most easy, most graceful exercise
that ever was used, and the most—   610

OLDFOX

Nay nay, sir, no more, sir, your servant; if you praise
martinet once, I have done with you, sir. Martinet!
Martinet!   *(Exit OLDFOX)*

FREEMAN

Nay, you have made him leave you as willingly as ever he
did an enemy, for he was truly for the king and parliament: 615
for the parliament in their list, and for the king in cheating
'em of their pay, and never hurting the king's party in the
field.

Enter a LAWYER *towards them*

MANLY

A pox, this way! Here's a lawyer I know threatening us with
another greeting.   620

598 *Gadsnouns* (By) God's (=Christ's) wounds
602 *broadsword* a short, old-fashioned sword; Oldfox's approval is not
surprising in view of his name
606 *martinet* the system of arms drill invented by General Jean Martinet,
a contemporary French drill-master and rigid disciplinarian; Captain
Wycherley was obliged to learn the exercise during the winter of
1673–4, when quartered with the fleet at Yarmouth on the Isle of
Wight during the third Anglo-Dutch war
616 *list* pay-roll

LAWYER

  Sir, sir, your very servant. I was afraid you had forgotten
  me.

MANLY

  I was not afraid you had forgotten me.

LAWYER

  No, sir; we lawyers have pretty good memories.

MANLY

  You ought to have, by your wits.   625

LAWYER

  O, you are a merry gentleman, sir; I remember you were
  merry when I was last in your company.

MANLY

  I was never merry in thy company, Master Lawyer, sure.

LAWYER

  Why, I'm sure you joked upon me and shammed me all night
  long.   630

MANLY

  Shammed! Prithee, what barbarous law term is that?

LAWYER

  Shamming? Why, don't you know that? 'Tis all our way of
  wit, sir.

MANLY

  I am glad I do not know it, then. Shamming!—What does he
  mean by't, Freeman?   635

FREEMAN

  Shamming is telling you an insipid, dull lie with a dull face,
  which the sly wag the author only laughs at himself; and
  making himself believe 'tis a good jest, puts the sham only
  upon himself.

MANLY

  So your lawyer's jest, I find, like his practice, has more   640
  knavery than wit in't. I should make the worst shammer in
  England. I must always deal ingenuously; as I will with you,
  Master Lawyer, and advise you to be seen rather with
  attorneys and solicitors than such fellows as I am; they will
  credit your practice more.   645

LAWYER

  No, sir; your company's an honour to me.

---

642 *ingenuously* Q6–7 (ingeniously Q1–5, 8, 0)

---

629 *shammed me* hoaxed me, 'sent me up'; cf. IV. ii, 24
645 *credit . . . more* do more credit to

MANLY

No, faith, go thy ways. There goes an attorney; leave me for
him. Let it be never said a lawyer's civility did him hurt.

LAWYER

No, worthy, honoured sir; I'll not leave you for any attorney,
sure.   650

MANLY

Unless he had a fee in his hand.

LAWYER

Have you any business here, sir? Try me. I'd serve you
sooner than any attorney breathing.

MANLY

Business? *(Aside)* So, I have thought of a sure way. [*Aloud*]
Yes, faith, I have a little business.   655

LAWYER

Have you so, sir? In what court, sir? What is't, sir? Tell me
but how I may serve you, and I'll do't, sir, and take it for
as great an honour—

MANLY

Faith, 'tis for a poor orphan of a sea officer of mine, that
has no money; but if it could be followed *in forma pauperis,*   660
and when the legacy's recovered—

LAWYER

Forma pauperis, sir?

MANLY

Ay, sir.

Several crossing the stage

LAWYER

Master Bumblecase, Master Bumblecase, a word with you.
[*To* MANLY] Sir, I beg your pardon at present; I have a little   665
business—

MANLY

Which is not *in forma pauperis.*   *(Exit* LAWYER*)*

FREEMAN

So, you have now found a way to be rid of people without
quarrelling.

Enter ALDERMAN

647 *thy ways* Q2–8 (this way Q1, 0)

660 *in forma pauperis* 'Is when any Man, who hath just cause of Sute in
Chancery, and . . . is not worth Five pounds, . . . shall have Council,
and Clerks assigned him, without paying Fees' (Blount)

MANLY

But here's a city rogue will stick as hard upon us as if I 670
owed him money.

ALDERMAN

Captain, noble sir, I am yours heartily, d'ye see. Why should
you avoid your old friends?

MANLY

And why should you follow me? I owe you nothing.

ALDERMAN

Out of my hearty respects to you, for there is not a man in 675
England—

MANLY

Thou wouldst save from hanging with the expense of a
shilling only.

ALDERMAN

Nay, nay; but captain, you are like enough to tell me—

MANLY

Truth, which you won't care to hear; therefore you had 680
better go talk with somebody else.

ALDERMAN

No; I know nobody can inform me better of some young wit
or spendthrift, that has a good dipped seat and estate in
Middlesex, Hertfordshire, Essex, or Kent; any of these would
serve my turn. Now, if you knew of such an one, and would 685
but help—

MANLY

You to finish his ruin.

ALDERMAN

I'faith, you should have a snip—

MANLY

Of your nose! You thirty in the hundred rascal, would you
make me your squire setter, you bawd for manors? 690

(Takes him by the nose)

ALDERMAN

O!

FREEMAN

Hold, or here will be your third lawsuit.

683 *dipped seat* mortgaged estate
688 *snip* share, cut
689 *thirty in the hundred rascal* money-lender charging 30 per cent
interest
690 *setter* a spy who informs thieves of suitable victims
690 *bawd* pimp

ALDERMAN

    Gadsprecious, you hectoring person you, are you wild? I
meant you no hurt, sir; I begin to think, as things go, land
security best, and have, for a convenient mortgage, some ten,   695
fifteen, or twenty thousand pound by me.

MANLY

    Then go lay it out upon an hospital and take a mortgage of
heaven, according to your city custom, for you think by
laying out a little money to hook in that too hereafter; do,
I say, and keep the poor you've made by taking forfeitures,   700
that heaven may not take yours.

ALDERMAN

    No, to keep the cripples you make this war; this war spoils
our trade.

MANLY

    Damn your trade; 'tis the better for't.

ALDERMAN

    What, will you speak against our trade?   705

MANLY

    And dare you speak against the war, our trade?

ALDERMAN

    (Aside) Well, he may be a convoy of ships I am concerned in.
[*Aloud*] Come, captain, I will have a fair correspondency
with you, say what you will.

MANLY

    Then prithee be gone.   710

ALDERMAN

    No, faith; prithee, captain, let's go drink a dish of laced
coffee, and talk of the times. Come, I'll treat you; nay, you
shall go, for I have no business here.

MANLY

    But I have.

ALDERMAN

    To pick up a man to give thee a dinner? Come, I'll do thy   715
business for thee.

MANLY

    Faith, now I think on't, so you may as well as any man; for

693 *Gadsprecious* (By) God's (=Christ's) precious (?blood)
693 *hectoring* bullying, domineering
697 *hospital* alms-house
707 *convoy* see I. 111 note
708 *have a fair correspondency* be on friendly terms
711–12 *laced coffee* 'Sugar'd' (*B.E.*) coffee

'tis to pick up a man to be bound with me to one who
expects city security, for—

ALDERMAN

Nay, then your servant, captain; business must be done.   **720**

MANLY

Ay, if it can; but hark you, alderman, without you—

ALDERMAN

Business, sir, I say, must be done;

Several crossing the stage

and there's an officer of the Treasury I have an affair with—
                                        (Exit ALDERMAN*)*

MANLY

You see now what the mighty friendship of the world is;
what all ceremony, embraces, and plentiful professions come   725
to. You are no more to believe a professing friend than a
threatening enemy; and as no man hurts you that tells you
he'll do you a mischief, no man, you see, is your servant
who says he is so. Why the devil, then, should a man be
troubled with the flattery of knaves, if he be not a fool or   730
cully; or with the fondness of fools, if he be not a knave or
cheat?

FREEMAN

Only for his pleasure; for there is some in laughing at fools
and disappointing knaves.

MANLY

That's a pleasure, I think, would cost you too dear, as well   735
as marrying your widow to disappoint her; but, for my part,
I have no pleasure by 'em but in despising 'em wheresoe'er I
meet 'em, and then the pleasure of hoping so to be rid of
'em. But now my comfort is, I am not worth a shilling in the
world, which all the world shall know; and then I'm sure I   740
shall have none of 'em come near me.

FREEMAN

A very pretty comfort, which I think you pay too dear for.
But is the twenty pound gone since the morning?

MANLY

To my boat's crew. Would you have the poor, honest, brave
fellows want?   745

FREEMAN

Rather than you or I.

725 *professions* promises, declarations
731 *fondness* silliness

MANLY

Why, art thou without money, thou who art a friend to everybody?

FREEMAN

I ventured my last stake upon the squire, to nick him of his mother, and cannot help you to a dinner, unless you will go 750 dine with my lord—

MANLY

No no; the ordinary is too dear for me where flattery must pay for my dinner. I am no herald, or poet.

FREEMAN

We'll go then to the bishop's—

MANLY

There you must flatter the old philosophy. I cannot renounce 755 my reason for a dinner.

FREEMAN

Why, then let's go to your alderman's.

MANLY

Hang him, rogue! That were not to dine, for he makes you drunk with lees of sack before dinner to take away your stomach; and there you must call usury and extortion God's 760 blessings, or the honest turning of the penny; hear him brag of the leather breeches in which he trotted first to town, and make a greater noise with his money in his parlour than his cashiers do in his counting-house, without hopes of borrowing a shilling.   765

FREEMAN

Ay, a pox on't; 'tis like dining with the great gamesters, and when they fall to their common dessert, see the heaps of gold drawn on all hands, without going to twelve. Let us go to my Lady Goodly's.

---

749 *nick him of* win him from
752–3 *the ordinary . . . dinner* i.e., I cannot afford my lord's table, which is like a public eating-house or *ordinary*, except that you pay with flattery instead of cash
753 *herald, or poet* two sycophants who fawn upon the nobility
755–6 *renounce my reason* The bishop's views are opposed to the fashionable new rationalism of Hobbes.
760 *stomach* appetite
767 *common dessert* i.e., their last course is gambling
768 *going to twelve* joining in with an equal share; cf. Shamwell in Shadwell's *The Squire of Alsatia* (1688): 'You Rogue, *Cheatly* . . . you will go to twelve with the Squire: If you do, I will have my snack' (V. i)
769 *Lady Goodly* here given a different character from that of II. 340–7.

MANLY

    There, to flatter her looks, you must mistake her grand-   770
children for her own, praise her cook that she may rail at
him, and feed her dogs, not yourself.

FREEMAN

    What d'ye think of eating with your lawyer, then?

MANLY

    Eat with him! Damn him; to hear him employ his barbarous
eloquence in a reading upon the two and thirty good bits in   775
a shoulder of veal, and be forced yourself to praise the cold
bribe pie that stinks, and drink law-French wine as rough and
harsh as his law-French. A pox on him, I'd rather dine in the
Temple Rounds or Walks with the knights without noses, or
the knights of the post, who are honester fellows and better   780
company. But let us home, and try our fortune; for I'll stay
no longer here for your damned widow.

FREEMAN

    Well, let us go home then; for I must go for my damned
widow, and look after my new damned charge. Three or four
hundred years ago, a man might have dined in this Hall.   785

MANLY

           But now the lawyer only here is fed,
           And, bully-like, by quarrels gets his bread.   *(Exeunt)*

Finis actus tertii

775 *reading* lecture
775–6 *the two . . . veal* from the proverb 'In a shoulder of *veal* there
    are twenty and two good bits'; in *A Collection of English Proverbs*
    (1678), John Ray explains that 'This is a piece of country wit. They
    mean by it, There are twenty (others say forty) bits in a shoulder of
    veal, and but two good ones' (p. 83)
779 *knights without noses* weather-beaten effigies of crusader knights in
    the Round of the Temple Church, where lawyers walked with
    clients and false witnesses plied for hire
785 *dined . . . Hall* where 'all the Kings of *England* since the Conquest
    . . . have . . . kept their Feasts, of Coronation especially; and other
    solemn Feasts, as at *Christmas,* and such like, most commonly'
    (John Stow, *A survey of . . . London,* ed. John Strype (1720), VI, 47);
    the last coronation breakfast here was that of George IV

Act IV, Scene i

MANLY'*s Lodging*

Enter MANLY *and* FIDELIA

MANLY

Well, there's success in thy face. Hast thou prevailed, say?

FIDELIA

As I could wish, sir.

MANLY

So; I told thee what thou wert fit for, and thou wouldst not
believe me. Come, thank me for bringing thee acquainted
with thy genius. Well, thou hast mollified her heart for me?   5

FIDELIA

No, sir, not so; but what's better.

MANLY

How! What's better?

FIDELIA

I shall harden your heart against her.

MANLY

Have a care, sir; my heart is too much in earnest to be
fooled with, and my desire at height and needs no delays to   10
incite it. What, you are too good a pimp already, and know
how to endear pleasure by withholding it? But leave off your
page's bawdy-house tricks, sir, and tell me, will she be kind?

FIDELIA

Kinder than you could wish, sir.

MANLY

So, then. Well, prithee, what said she?   15

FIDELIA

She said—

MANLY

What? Thou'rt so tedious; speak comfort to me. What?

FIDELIA

That, of all things, you were her aversion.

MANLY

How!

18 *were* Q1 (are Q2–8, 0)

---

5 *genius* special ability

14 *Kinder* Fidelia puns on *kind* (1) benevolent (2) true to her own
nature, i.e., lecherous

FIDELIA

That she would sooner take a bedfellow out of an hospital,   20
and diseases, into her arms than you.

MANLY

What?

FIDELIA

That she would rather trust her honour with a dissolute,
debauched hector; nay, worse, with a finical, baffled coward,
all over loathsome with affectation of the fine gentleman.   25

MANLY

What's all this you say?

FIDELIA

Nay, that my offers of your love to her were more offensive
than when parents woo their virgin daughters to the enjoy-
ment of riches only, and that you were in all circumstances
as nauseous to her as a husband on compulsion.   30

MANLY

Hold; I understand you not.

FIDELIA *(Aside)*

So, 'twill work, I see.

MANLY

Did not you tell me—

FIDELIA

She called you ten thousand ruffians.

MANLY

Hold, I say.   35

FIDELIA

Brutes—

MANLY

Hold.

FIDELIA

Sea monsters—

MANLY

Damn your intelligence! Hear me a little now.

FIDELIA

Nay, surly coward she called you too.   40

MANLY

Won't you hold yet? Hold, or—

FIDELIA

Nay, sir, pardon me; I could not but tell you she had the

24 *hector* 'a Vaporing, Swaggering Coward' (*B.E.*)
24 *finical, baffled* over-nice, disgraced
39 *intelligence* information, news

baseness, the injustice, to call you coward, sir; coward, coward, sir.

MANLY

Not yet? 45

FIDELIA

I've done. Coward, sir.

MANLY

Did not you say she was kinder than I could wish her?

FIDELIA

Yes, sir.

MANLY

How then?—O, I understand you now. At first she appeared in rage and disdain, the truest sign of a coming woman; but 50 at last you prevailed, it seems; did you not?

FIDELIA

Yes, sir.

MANLY

So then, let's know that only. Come, prithee, without delays. I'll kiss thee for that news beforehand.

FIDELIA *(Aside)*

So; the kiss, I'm sure, is welcome to me, whatsoe'er the news 55 will be to you.

MANLY

Come, speak, my dear volunteer.

FIDELIA *(Aside)*

How welcome were that kind word too, if it were not for another woman's sake!

MANLY

What, won't you speak? You prevailed for me at last, you 60 say?

FIDELIA

No, sir.

MANLY

No more of your fooling, sir; it will not agree with my impatience or temper.

FIDELIA

Then, not to fool you, sir, I spoke to her for you, but pre- 65 vailed for myself. She would not hear me when I spoke in your behalf, but bid me say what I would in my own, though she gave me no occasion, she was so coming, and so was

50 *coming* eager
54 *I'll kiss thee* see II. 288 note; Farquhar repeats this situation when Plume kisses 'Jack Wilful' in IV. i of *The Recruiting Officer* (1706)

kinder, sir, than you could wish; which I was only afraid to
let you know without some warning.   70

MANLY

How's this? Young man, you are of a lying age; but I must
hear you out, and if—

FIDELIA

I would not abuse you, and cannot wrong her by any report
of her, she is so wicked.

MANLY

How, wicked! Had she the impudence, at the second sight   75
of you only—

FIDELIA

Impudence, sir? O, she has impudence enough to put a court
out of countenance and debauch a stews.

MANLY

Why, what said she?

FIDELIA

Her tongue, I confess, was silent; but her speaking eyes   80
gloated such things, more immodest and lascivious than
ravishers can act or women under a confinement think.

MANLY

I know there are whose eyes reflect more obscenity than the
glasses in alcoves, but there are others too who use a little
art with their looks to make 'em seem more beautiful, not   85
more loving; which vain young fellows like you are apt to
interpret in their own favour and to the lady's wrong.

FIDELIA

Seldom, sir; pray, have you a care of gloating eyes; for he
that loves to gaze upon 'em will find at last a thousand fools
and cuckolds in 'em, instead of cupids.   90

MANLY

Very well, sir; but what, you had only eye-kindness from
Olivia?

FIDELIA

I tell you again, sir, no woman sticks there. Eye-promises of
love they only keep; nay, they are contracts which make you
sure of 'em. In short, sir, she, seeing me with shame and   95

84 *others too* Q1, 0 (others Q2–8)

---

78 *stews* brothel
81 *gloated such things* made amorous promises (see II. 71; 'such things'
   is perhaps a cognate object)
82 *under a confinement* in child-bed (not cited in *OED* before 1774)
84 *glasses in alcoves* bedroom mirrors

amazement dumb, unactive, and resistless, threw her twisting arms about my neck and smothered me with a thousand tasteless kisses; believe me, sir, they were so to me.

MANLY

Why did you not avoid 'em, then?

FIDELIA

I fenced with her eager arms as you did with the grapples of   100
the enemy's fire-ship, and nothing but cutting 'em off could have freed me.

MANLY

Damned, damned woman, that could be so false and in-famous! And damned, damned heart of mine, that cannot yet be false, though so infamous! What easy, tame, suffering,   105
trampled things does that little god of talking cowards make of us! But—

FIDELIA *(Aside)*

So! It works, I find, as I expected.

MANLY

But she was false to me before; she told me so herself, and yet I could not quite believe it; but she was, so that her second   110
falseness is a favour to me, not an injury, in revenging me upon the man that wronged me first of her love. Her love! A whore's, a witch's love!—But what, did she not kiss well, sir? I'm sure I thought her lips—but I must not think of 'em more; but yet they are such I could still kiss, grow to—and   115
then tear off with my teeth, grind 'em into mammocks, and spit 'em into her cuckold's face.

FIDELIA *(Aside)*

Poor man, how uneasy he is! I have hardly the heart to give him so much pain, though withal I give him a cure, and to myself new life.   120

MANLY

But what, her kisses sure could not but warm you into desire at last, or a compliance with hers at least?

FIDELIA

Nay more, I confess—

98 *tasteless* insipid
101 *fire-ship* (1) a burning ship, set adrift amongst others to destroy them, hence (2) 'a Pockey Whore' (*B.E.*), a pardonable overstate-ment by Fidelia
115 *still kiss* go on kissing
116 *mammocks* shreds, little torn pieces

MANLY

What more? Speak.

FIDELIA

All you could fear had passed between us, if I could have   125
been made to wrong you, sir, in that nature.

MANLY

Could have been made? You lie; you did.

FIDELIA

Indeed, sir, 'twas impossible for me; besides, we were interrupted by a visit. But, I confess, she would not let me stir
till I promised to return to her again within this hour, as   130
soon as it should be dark, by which time she would dispose
of her visit and her servants and herself for my reception;
which I was fain to promise, to get from her.

MANLY

Ha!

FIDELIA

But if ever I go near her again, may you, sir, think me as   135
false to you as she is; hate and renounce me, as you ought to
do her and, I hope, will do now.

MANLY

Well, but now I think on't, you shall keep your word with
your lady. What, a young fellow, and fail the first, nay, so
tempting an assignation!   140

FIDELIA

How, sir?

MANLY

I say you shall go to her when 'tis dark, and shall not disappoint her.

FIDELIA

I, sir! I should disappoint her more by going, for—

MANLY

How so?   145

FIDELIA

Her impudence and injustice to you will make me disappoint
her love, loathe her.

MANLY

Come, you have my leave; and if you disgust her, I'll go with
you and act love, whilst you shall talk it only.

FIDELIA

You, sir! Nay, then I'll never go near her. You act love, sir!   150

133 *fain* obliged, under the circumstances
148 *disgust* dislike

You must but act it indeed, after all I have said to you.
Think of your honour, sir. Love—

MANLY

Well, call it revenge, and that is honourable. I'll be revenged
on her; and thou shalt be my second.

FIDELIA

Not in a base action, sir, when you are your own enemy. O,   155
go not near her, sir; for heaven's sake, for your own, think
not of it!

MANLY

How concerned you are! I thought I should catch you. What,
you are my rival at last and are in love with her yourself;
and have spoken ill of her out of your love to her, not me;   160
and therefore would not have me go to her!

FIDELIA

Heaven witness for me, 'tis because I love you only I would
not have you go to her.

MANLY

Come, come, the more I think on't, the more I'm satisfied
you do love her. Those kisses, young man, I knew were   165
irresistible; 'tis certain.

FIDELIA

There is nothing certain in the world, sir, but my truth and
your courage.

MANLY

Your servant, sir. Besides, false and ungrateful as she has
been to me, and though I may believe her hatred to me great   170
as you report it, yet I cannot think you are so soon and at
that rate beloved by her, though you may endeavour it.

FIDELIA

Nay, if that be all and you doubt it still, sir, I will conduct
you to her and, unseen, your ears shall judge of her falseness and my truth to you, if that will satisfy you.   175

MANLY

Yes, there is some satisfaction in being quite out of doubt,
because 'tis that alone withholds us from the pleasure of
revenge.

FIDELIA

Revenge! What revenge can you have, sir? Disdain is best
revenged by scorn, and faithless love by loving another and   180

169 *Your servant, sir* I disagree, sir; see II. 271 note

making her happy with the other's losings; which, if I might advise—

Enter FREEMAN

MANLY

Not a word more.

FREEMAN

What, are you talking of love yet, captain? I thought you had done with't.   185

MANLY

Why, what did you hear me say?

FREEMAN

Something imperfectly of love, I think.

MANLY

I was only wondering why fools, rascals, and desertless wretches should still have the better of men of merit with all women, as much as with their own common mistress, fortune.   190

FREEMAN

Because most women, like fortune, are blind, seem to do all things in jest, and take pleasure in extravagant actions; their love deserves neither thanks or blame, for they cannot help it; 'tis all sympathy. Therefore the noisy, the finical, the talkative, the cowardly and effeminate have the better of the   195 brave, the reasonable, and man of honour, for they have no more reason in their love or kindness than fortune herself.

MANLY

Yes, they have their reason. First, honour in a man they fear too much to love, and sense in a lover upbraids their want of it; and they hate anything that disturbs their admira-   200 tion of themselves. But they are of that vain number who had rather show their false generosity in giving away pro- fusely to worthless flatterers than in paying just debts; and, in short, all women, like fortune, as you say, and rewards, are lost by too much meriting.   205

FIDELIA

All women, sir? Sure, there are some who have no other quarrel to a lover's merit but that it begets their despair of him.

MANLY

Thou art young enough to be credulous, but we—

Enter FIRST SAILOR

194 *finical* over-fastidious

1 SAILOR

Here are now below the scolding, daggled gentlewoman and   210
that Major Old—Old—fop, I think you call him.

FREEMAN

Oldfox. Prithee, bid 'em come up—with your leave, captain,
for now I can talk with her upon the square, if I shall not
disturb you.   [*Exit* SAILOR]

MANLY

No, for I'll be gone. Come, volunteer.   215

FREEMAN

Nay, pray stay; the scene between us will not be so tedious
to you as you think. Besides, you shall see how I have rigged
my squire out with the remains of my shipwrecked wardrobe; he is under your sea valet-de-chambre's hands, and by
this time dressed, and will be worth your seeing. Stay, and   220
I'll fetch my fool.

MANLY

No; you know I cannot easily laugh. Besides, my volunteer
and I have business abroad.

> (*Exeunt* MANLY, FIDELIA *on one side,* FREEMAN *on t'other*)

> *Enter* MAJOR OLDFOX *and* WIDOW BLACKACRE

WIDOW

What, nobody here! Did not the fellow say he was within?

OLDFOX

Yes, lady; and he may be perhaps a little busy at present; but   225
if you think the time long till he comes, *(Unfolding papers)*
I'll read you here some of the fruits of my leisure, the over-
flowings of my fancy and pen. *(Aside)* To value me right, she
must know my parts. [*Aloud*] Come—

WIDOW

No no, I have reading work enough of my own in my bag,   230
I thank you.

OLDFOX

Ay, law, madam; but here is a poem in blank verse, which
I think a handsome declaration of one's passion.

WIDOW

O, if you talk of declarations, I'll show you one of the

210 *daggled* spattered with mud
213 *upon the square* openly, directly (since Jerry is now under his con-
      trol)
223 s.d. *Enter* . . . BLACKACRE With two permanent doors on each side
      of the forestage, there is no risk of an unwanted meeting here.
234 *declarations* papers 'shewing in writing the grief of the Demandant
      or Plaintife against the Tenent or Defendant' (Phillips)

prettiest penned things, which I mended too myself, you must   235
know.

OLDFOX

Nay, lady, if you have used yourself so much to the reading
of harsh law that you hate smooth poetry, here is a character
for you of—

WIDOW

A character! Nay, then I'll show you my bill in chancery   240
here, that gives you such a character of my adversary, makes
him as black—

OLDFOX

Pshaw; away, away, lady. But if you think the character too
long, here is an epigram, not above twenty lines, upon a cruel
lady who decreed her servant should hang himself to demon-   245
strate his passion.

WIDOW

Decreed! If you talk of decreeing, I have such a decree here,
drawn by the finest clerk—

OLDFOX

O lady, lady, all interruption and no sense between us, as if
we were lawyers at the bar! But I had forgot, Apollo and   250
Littleton never lodge in a head together. If you hate verses,
I'll give you a cast of my politics in prose. 'Tis a letter to a
friend in the country, which is now the way of all such
sober, solid persons as myself, when they have a mind to
publish their disgust to the times; though perhaps, between   255
you and I, they have no friend in the country. And sure a
politic, serious person may as well have a feigned friend in
the country to write to, as well as an idle poet a feigned

237 *used* accustomed
238 *character* short prose portrait, usually satiric, of a well-known type:
     miser, hypocrite, choleric man, etc.
245 *servant* professed lover
245–6 *hang . . . passion* an unwitting *double entendre*: hanging gave a
     man an erection
247 *decree* the judgment of an equity court, as in II. 853
250–1 *Apollo and Littleton* i.e., poetry and law; Sir Thomas Littleton's
     Tenures (1481), translated from law-French into English in 1525, and
     with the commentary by Sir Edward Coke added in 1628, had been
     reprinted as recently as 1671.
252 *cast* specimen
255 *disgust* aversion
256 *you and I* common usage at this period; cf. 'Let you and I tickle
     him' (*The Country Wife* (1675), IV. iii, 79)

mistress to write to. And so here's my *Letter to a Friend* (or
no friend) *in the Country, concerning the late conjuncture of*   260
affairs in relation to Coffee-houses; or, the Coffee-man's Case.
WIDOW

Nay, if your letter have a case in't, 'tis something; but first
I'll read you a letter of mine to a friend in the country,
called a letter of attorney.

> *Enter to them* FREEMAN *and* JERRY BLACKACRE *in an old*
> *gaudy suit and red breeches of Freeman's*

OLDFOX *(Aside)*

What, interruption still? O the plague of interruption, worse   265
to an author than the plague of critics!
WIDOW

What's this I see, Jerry Blackacre my minor in red breeches!
—What, hast thou left the modest, seemly garb of gown and
cap for this? And have I lost all my good Inns of Chancery
breeding upon thee, then? And thou wilt go a-breeding   270
thyself from our Inn of Chancery and Westminster Hall, at
coffee-houses and ordinaries, playhouses, tennis courts, and
bawdy-houses?
JERRY

Ay ay, what then? Perhaps I will; but what's that to you?
Here's my guardian and tutor now, forsooth, that I am out   275
of your huckster's hands.

---

259 *here's* Q2–8, 0 (here is Q1)

259–61 *Letter . . . Case* Supposedly, one of many pamphlets attacking
the royal proclamation of 29 December 1675/6 to suppress coffee-
houses as 'places where the disaffected met, and spread scandalous
reports concerning the conduct of His Majesty and His Ministers'
(B. Lillywhite, *London Coffee Houses* (1963), p. 18); the public
outcry was so great it was never put into effect.
264 *letter of attorney* formal document whereby 'any friend made choice
of for that purpose, is appointed to do a lawful act in anothers
stead' (Phillips)
264 s.d. *suit* here, matching coat and waistcoat
269 *Inns of Chancery* see I. 418–19 note
272 *ordinaries* public eating-houses, often used for gambling; the other
locations are also rakish haunts; cf. Vincent to Ranger in Wycherley's *Love in a Wood* (1671): 'I was going to look you out, between
the Scenes at the Play-House, the Coffee-house, Tennis-Court, or
Gifford's', a notorious brothel (IV. iii)
275–6 *out . . . hands* free from your disastrous usage; cf. '*In Huckster's
Hands,* at a desperate Pass, or Condition, or in a fair way to be
Lost' (*B.E.*)

WIDOW

How? Thou hast not chosen him for thy guardian yet?

JERRY

No, but he has chosen me for his charge, and that's all one;
and I'll do anything he'll have me, and go all the world over
with him, to ordinaries and bawdy-houses, or anywhere else. 280

WIDOW

To ordinaries and bawdy-houses! Have a care, minor; thou
wilt enfeeble there thy estate and body. Do not go to
ordinaries and bawdy-houses, good Jerry.

JERRY

Why, how come you to know any ill by bawdy-houses? You
never had any hurt by 'em, had you, forsooth? Pray hold 285
yourself contented; if I do go where money and wenches are
to be had, you may thank yourself, for you used me so
unnaturally you would never let me have a penny to go
abroad with, nor so much as come near the garret where
your maidens lay; nay, you would not so much as let me play 290
at hot cockles with 'em, nor have any recreation with 'em,
though one should have kissed you behind, you were so
unnatural a mother, so you were.

FREEMAN

Ay, a very unnatural mother, faith, squire.

WIDOW

But, Jerry, consider thou art yet but a minor; however, if 295
thou wilt go home with me again and be a good child, thou
shalt see—

FREEMAN

Madam, I must have a better care of my heir under age than
so; I would sooner trust him alone with a stale waiting-
woman and a parson, than with his widow mother and her 300
lover or lawyer.

WIDOW

Why, thou villain, part mother and minor! Rob me of my
child and my writings! But thou shalt find there's law, and

278 *all one* the same thing
290 *maidens* maid-servants
291 *hot cockles* a childish game where one player lies face downwards
and tries to guess who hits his back
292 *kissed you behind* followed you meekly (?); cf. I. 10–11
299 *stale* i.e., past her prime

as in the case of ravishment of guard: Westminster the
Second. 305
OLDFOX

Young gentleman, squire, pray be ruled by your mother and
your friends.
JERRY

Yes, I'll be ruled by my friends, therefore not by my mother,
so I won't. I'll choose him for my guardian till I am of age;
nay, maybe for as long as I live. 310
WIDOW

Wilt thou so, thou wretch? And when thou'rt of age, thou
wilt sign, seal, and deliver too, wilt thou?
JERRY

Yes, marry will I, if you go there too.
WIDOW

O do not squeeze wax, son; rather go to ordinaries and
bawdy-houses than squeeze wax. If thou dost that, farewell 315
the goodly manor of Blackacre, with all its woods, underwoods, and appurtenances whatever. O, O! *(Weeps)*
FREEMAN

Come, madam; in short, you see I am resolved to have a
share in the estate, yours or your son's; if I cannot get you,
I'll keep him, who is less coy, you find; but if you would 320
have your son again, you must take me too. Peace or war?
Love or law? You see my hostage is in my hand; I'm in
possession.
WIDOW

Nay, if one of us must be ruined, e'en let it be him. By my
body, a good one! Did you ever know yet a widow marry 325

304–5 *Westminster the Second* Chapter 35 of the statute known as Westminster 2 (1285) provided legal remedy against the abduction of a
ward (ravishment de gard)
313 *go there* come to that (also at 343 and 351)
314 *squeeze wax* set seal to a document (and so be permanently bound
by it)
316–17 *underwoods* stretches of brushwood, etc. growing beneath tall
timber
317 *appurtenances* things belonging to something more principal, 'as
Hamlets to a cheif Mannor, Common of Pasture, Turbary, Piscary,
and such like' (Blount)
322 *in my hand* led by my will
325 *a good one* ironic comment on an improbable statement, cf. 'That's
a good one' in *The Country Wife* (1675, III. ii, 204); *OED* notes
'that's a good 'un' as 'early 19th-century slang'

or not marry for the sake of her child? I'd have you to
know, sir, I shall be hard enough for you both yet, without
marrying you, if Jerry won't be ruled by me.—What say
you, booby, will you be ruled? Speak.

JERRY

Let one alone, can't you?   330

WIDOW

Wilt thou choose him for guardian whom I refuse for
husband?

JERRY

Ay, to choose, I thank you.

WIDOW

And are all my hopes frustrated? Shall I never hear thee put
cases again to John the butler, or our vicar? Never see thee   335
amble the circuit with the judges, and hear thee, in our town
hall, louder than the crier?

JERRY

No, for I have taken my leave of lawyering and pettifogging.

WIDOW

Pettifogging! Thou profane villain, hast thou so? Pettifogging! Then you shall take your leave of me and your   340
estate too; thou shalt be an alien to me and it forever.
Pettifogging!

JERRY

O, but if you go there too, mother, we have the deeds and
settlements, I thank you. Would you cheat me of my estate,
i'fac?   345

WIDOW

No no, I will not cheat your little brother Bob; for thou
wert not born in wedlock.

FREEMAN

How's that?

JERRY

How? What quirk has she got in her head now?

WIDOW

I say thou canst not, shalt not inherit the Blackacre's estate.   350

JERRY

Why? Why, forsooth? What d'ye mean, if you go there too?

WIDOW

Thou art but my base child, and according to the law canst

351 *too* Q2–8, 0 (to Q1)

352 *base* illegitimate

F

not inherit it; nay, thou art not so much as bastard eigne.

JERRY

What, what? Am I then the son of a whore, mother?

WIDOW

The law says—   355

FREEMAN

Madam, we know what the law says; but have a care what
you say. Do not let your passion to ruin your son ruin your
reputation.

WIDOW

Hang reputation, sir! Am not I a widow, have no husband,
nor intend to have any? Nor would you, I suppose, now   360
have me for a wife. So I think now I'm revenged on my son
and you, without marrying, as I told you.

FREEMAN

But consider, madam.

JERRY

What, have you no shame left in you, mother?

WIDOW *(Aside, to* OLDFOX*)*

Wonder not at it, major; 'tis often the poor pressed widow's   365
case, to give up her honour to save her jointure, and seem to
be a light woman rather than marry; as some young men,
they say, pretend to have the filthy disease, and lose credit
with most women to avoid the importunities of some.

FREEMAN

But one word with you, madam.   370

WIDOW

No no, sir.—Come, major, let us make haste now to the
Prerogative Court.

OLDFOX

But, lady, if what you say be true, will you stigmatize your
reputation on record? And if it be not true, how will you
prove it?   375

WIDOW

Pshaw! I can prove anything; and for my reputation, know,
major, a wise woman will no more value her reputation in
disinheriting a rebellious son of a good estate, than she would
in getting him, to inherit an estate.

(Exeunt WIDOW *and* OLDFOX*)*

353 *bastard eigne* bastard son of parents who later marry and have a
legitimate son
372 *Prerogative Court* an archbishop's court which 'sits upon Inheri-
tances fallen either by the Intestate, or by Will and Testament'
(Phillips)

FREEMAN

Madam!—We must not let her go so, squire.   380

JERRY

Nay, the devil can't stop her though, if she has a mind to't.
But come, bully guardian, we'll go and advise with three
attorneys, two proctors, two solicitors, and a shrewd man of
Whitefriars, neither attorney, proctor, or solicitor, but as pure
a pimp to the law as any of 'em; and sure all they will be   385
hard enough for her, for I fear, bully guardian, you are too
good a joker to have any law in your head.

FREEMAN

Thou'rt in the right on't, squire; I understand no law,
especially that against bastards, since I'm sure the custom is
against that law, and more people get estates by being so   390
than lose 'em.   *(Exeunt)*

[Act IV, Scene ii]

The scene changes to OLIVIA'*s Lodging*

Enter LORD PLAUSIBLE, *and* BOY *with a candle*

LORD PLAUSIBLE

Little gentleman, your most obedient, faithful, humble
servant. Where, I beseech you, is that divine person, your
noble lady?

BOY

Gone out, my lord; but commanded me to give you this
letter.   *(Gives him a letter)*   5

Enter to him NOVEL

383 *attorneys . . . solicitors* Proctors managed their clients' causes in
courts of civil or canon law, attorneys and solicitors in courts of
common law and chancery.

384 *Whitefriars* site of a dissolved convent near Fleet Street, which re-
tained until 1697 privilege of sanctuary, and consequently harboured
many criminals and their aides

s.d. *scene changes* i.e., the wings and back scene slide away on
shutters to reveal others depicting Olivia's rooms, all in full view
of the audience

s.d. *with a candle* to suggest that the scene is played by its light,
though the theatre remained fully illuminated throughout the performance; when the candle is removed (102), the characters are left
'in the dark' (107) until Vernish re-enters '*with a light*' (354); the
same convention is employed in V, iii

LORD PLAUSIBLE *(Aside)*

Which he must not observe.   *(Puts it up)*

NOVEL

Hey, boy, where is thy lady?

BOY

Gone out, sir; but I must beg a word with you.

(Gives him a letter, and exit)

NOVEL

For me? So. *(Puts up the letter)*—Servant, servant, my lord.
You see the lady knew of your coming, for she is gone out.   10

LORD PLAUSIBLE

Sir, I humbly beseech you not to censure the lady's good
breeding; she has reason to use more liberty with me than
with any other man.

NOVEL

How, viscount, how?

LORD PLAUSIBLE

Nay, I humbly beseech you, be not in choler; where there is   15
most love, there may be most freedom.

NOVEL

Nay, then 'tis time to come to an *éclaircissement* with you,
and to tell you, you must think no more of this lady's love.

LORD PLAUSIBLE

Why, under correction, dear sir?

NOVEL

There are reasons, reasons, viscount.   20

LORD PLAUSIBLE

What, I beseech you, noble sir?

NOVEL

Prithee, prithee, be not impertinent, my lord; some of you
lords are such conceited, well-assured, impertinent rogues.

LORD PLAUSIBLE

And you noble wits are so full of shamming and drolling
one knows not where to have you, seriously.   25

NOVEL

Well, you shall find me in bed with this lady one of these
days.

---

17 *éclaircissement* explanation (also at 33); the word is affected by
Melantha in Dryden's *Marriage à la Mode* (1671, V. i) and the fop
Sparkish in *The Country Wife* (1675, III. ii, 285)

24 *shamming* hoaxing; see III. 629–39

26 *in bed with this lady* On the wedding night, bride and groom were
put to bed by their friends, who awakened them next morning with
a sack-posset; Plausible pretends to misunderstand Novel here.

LORD PLAUSIBLE
  Nay, I beseech you, spare the lady's honour; for hers and
  mine will be all one shortly.
NOVEL
  Prithee, my lord, be not an ass. Dost thou think to get her   30
  from me? I have had such good encouragements—
LORD PLAUSIBLE
  I have not been thought unworthy of 'em.
NOVEL
  What, not like mine! Come to an *éclaircissement*, as I said.
LORD PLAUSIBLE
  Why, seriously then, she has told me viscountess sounded
  prettily.   35
NOVEL
  And me, that Novel was a name she would sooner change
  hers for than for any title in England.
LORD PLAUSIBLE
  She has commended the softness and respectfulness of my
  behaviour.
NOVEL
  She has praised the briskness of my raillery of all things,   40
  man.
LORD PLAUSIBLE
  The sleepiness of my eyes she liked.
NOVEL
  Sleepiness! Dullness, dullness. But the fierceness of mine
  she adored.
LORD PLAUSIBLE
  The brightness of my hair she liked.   45
NOVEL
  The brightness! No, the greasiness, I warrant. But the black-
  ness and lustre of mine she admires.
LORD PLAUSIBLE
  The gentleness of my smile.
NOVEL
  The subtlety of my leer.
LORD PLAUSIBLE
  The clearness of my complexion.   50
NOVEL
  The redness of my lips.
LORD PLAUSIBLE
  The whiteness of my teeth.

  31 *such good* Q2–8 (such Q1, 0)

NOVEL

My janty way of picking them.

LORD PLAUSIBLE

The sweetness of my breath.

NOVEL

Ha ha! Nay, then she abused you, 'tis plain; for you know   55
what Manly said. The sweetness of your pulvilio she might
mean, but for your breath! Ha ha ha! Your breath is such,
man, that nothing but tobacco can perfume, and your complexion nothing could mend but the smallpox.

LORD PLAUSIBLE

Well, sir, you may please to be merry; but, to put you out of   60
all doubt, sir, she has received some jewels from me of value.

NOVEL

And presents from me, besides what I presented her jantily,
by way of ombre, of three or four hundred pound value,
which I'm sure are the earnest pence for our love bargain.

LORD PLAUSIBLE

Nay then, sir, with your favour, and to make an end of all   65
your hopes, look you there, sir, she has writ to me—

NOVEL

How! How! Well, well, and so she has to me; look you
there—   *([They] deliver to each other their letters)*

LORD PLAUSIBLE

What's here!

NOVEL

How's this? *(Reads out)* 'My dear lord, You'll excuse me for   70
breaking my word with you, since 'twas to oblige, not offend
you, for I am only gone abroad but to disappoint Novel and
meet you in the drawing-room, where I expect you with as
much impatience as when I used to suffer Novel's visits, the
most impertinent fop that ever affected the name of a wit,   75
therefore not capable, I hope, to give you jealousy; for, for
your sake alone, you saw I renounced an old lover, and will
do all the world. Burn the letter, but lay up the kindness of
it in your heart, with your Olivia'.—Very fine! But pray let's
see mine.   80

---

53 *janty* well-bred, genteel, elegant
56 *what Manly said* in II. 571–3
56 *pulvilio* perfumed powder for dressing wigs
64 *earnest pence* a small sum paid as deposit to secure a bargain
73 *drawing-room* at Whitehall; see II. 81 note

LORD PLAUSIBLE

I understand it not; but sure she cannot think so of me.

NOVEL

(Reads the other letter) Hum! Ha!—'meet—for your sake'
—umh!—'quitted an old lover—world—burn—in your
heart, with your Olivia'.—Just the same, the names only
altered.   85

LORD PLAUSIBLE

Surely there must be some mistake, or somebody has abused
her and us.

NOVEL

Yes, you are abused, no doubt on't, my lord; but I'll to
Whitehall and see.

LORD PLAUSIBLE

And I, where I shall find you are abused.   90

NOVEL

Where, if it be so, for our comfort we cannot fail of meeting
with fellow-sufferers enough; for, as Freeman said of another,
she stands in the drawing-room like the glass, ready for all
comers to set their gallantry by her, and, like the glass too,
lets no man go from her unsatisfied with himself.   95

(Exeunt ambo)

Enter OLIVIA *and* BOY

OLIVIA

Both here, and just gone?

BOY

Yes, madam.

OLIVIA

But are you sure neither saw you deliver the other a letter?

BOY

Yes yes, madam, I am very sure.

OLIVIA

Go then to the Old Exchange, to Westminster, Holborn,   100
and all the other places I told you of; I shall not need you
these two hours. Be gone, and take the candle with you; and
be sure you leave word again below, I am gone out to all
that ask.

---

84 *Just the same* not quite, since 'quitted' is substituted for 'renounced'

100 *Old . . . Holborn* i.e., all over town, from Westminster at its south-
west boundary to Holborn in the north and the Royal Exchange in
Cornhill, deep in the city

BOY

Yes, madam.   *(Exit)*   105

OLIVIA

And my new lover will not ask, I'm sure. He has his lesson,
and cannot miss me here, though in the dark, which I have
purposely designed as a remedy against my blushing gallant's modesty; for young lovers, like game cocks, are made
bolder by being kept without light.   110

Enter her husband VERNISH, *as from a journey*

VERNISH

Where is she? Darkness everywhere!

OLIVIA *(Softly)*

What, come before your time? My soul! My life! Your
haste has augmented your kindness, and let me thank you for
it thus, and thus—*(Embracing and kissing him)*. And though,
my soul, the little time since you left me has seemed an age   115
to my impatience, sure it is yet but seven—

VERNISH

How! Who's that you expected after seven?

OLIVIA *(Aside)*

Ha! My husband returned! And have I been throwing away
so many kind kisses on my husband, and wronged my lover
already?   120

VERNISH

Speak, I say, who was't you expected after seven?

OLIVIA

(Aside) What shall I say? O! [*Aloud*] Why, 'tis but seven
days, is it, dearest, since you went out of town? And I
expected you not so soon.

VERNISH

No, sure, 'tis but five days since I left you.   125

OLIVIA

Pardon my impatience, dearest; I thought 'em seven at least.

VERNISH

Nay, then—

118 s.d. *(Aside)* Q2–8 *(omitted* Q1, 0)

---

109 *game cocks* cocks trained for fighting; since game (=amorous play)
   and cock (=penis) are well-established *double entendres,* it is likely
   that *game cock* itself, first recorded by *OED* in this passage, is also
   equivocal

111 s.d. *(Softly)* placed between 111 and 112 in Q1; Olivia's mistake is
   more plausible if Vernish speaks softly, but since she speaks softly
   to Fidelia at 177, she probably does so here as well

OLIVIA

But, my life, you shall never stay half so long from me again;
you shan't indeed, by this kiss, you shan't.

VERNISH

No no; but why alone in the dark?   130

OLIVIA

Blame not my melancholy in your absence. But, my soul,
since you went, I have strange news to tell you: Manly is
returned.

VERNISH

Manly returned! Fortune forbid!

OLIVIA

Met with the Dutch in the Channel, fought, sunk his ship   135
and all he carried with him. He was here with me yesterday.

VERNISH

And did you own our marriage to him?

OLIVIA

I told him I was married, to put an end to his love and my
trouble; but to whom is yet a secret kept from him and all
the world. And I have used him so scurvily his great spirit   140
will ne'er return to reason it farther with me; I have sent him
to sea again, I warrant.

VERNISH

'Twas bravely done. And sure he will now hate the shore
more than ever, after so great a disappointment. Be you sure
only to keep awhile our great secret till he be gone. In the   145
mean time, I'll lead the easy, honest fool by the nose, as I
used to do; and whilst he stays, rail with him at thee, and
when he's gone, laugh with thee at him. But have you his
cabinet of jewels safe? Part not with a seed pearl to him to
keep him from starving.   150

OLIVIA

Nor from hanging.

VERNISH

He cannot recover 'em and, I think, will scorn to beg 'em
again.

OLIVIA

But, my life, have you taken the thousand guineas he left in
my name out of the goldsmith's hands?   155

VERNISH

Ay ay, they are removed to another goldsmith's.

152 *recover 'em* obtain possession of them by legal process
155 *goldsmith* who doubled as banker at this period; we learn at 409 he
    is also an alderman

OLIVIA

Ay, but, my soul, you had best have a care he find not where
the money is; for his present wants, as I'm informed, are
such as will make him inquisitive enough.

VERNISH

You say true, and he knows the man too; but I'll remove it   160
tomorrow.

OLIVIA

Tomorrow! O do not stay till tomorrow; go tonight,
immediately.

VERNISH

Now I think on't, you advise well, and I will go presently.

OLIVIA

Presently? Instantly! I will not let you stay a jot.   165

VERNISH

I will then, though I return not home till twelve.

OLIVIA

Nay, though not till morning, with all my heart. Go, dearest;
I am impatient till you are gone.   *(Thrusts him out)*
So, I have at once now brought about those two grateful
businesses which all prudent women do together, secured   170
money and pleasure; and now all interruptions of the last
are removed. Go husband, and come up friend; just the
buckets in the well: the absence of one brings the other; but
I hope, like them too, they will not meet in the way, justle,
and clash together.   175

Enter FIDELIA, *and* MANLY *treading softly and staying behind
at some distance*

So, are you come? [*Aside*] But not the husband-bucket, I
hope, again. *(Softly)* Who's there? My dearest?

FIDELIA

My life—

OLIVIA

Right, right. Where are thy lips? Here, take the dumb and
best welcomes, kisses and embraces; 'tis not a time for idle   180
words. In a duel of love, as in others, parleying shows
basely. Come, we are alone, and now the word is only satisfaction, and defend not thyself.

MANLY *(Aside)*

How's this? Wuh, she makes love like a devil in a play; and

169 *grateful* welcome, agreeable
172 *friend* lover

in this darkness, which conceals her angel's face, if I were   185
apt to be afraid, I should think her a devil.

OLIVIA

What, you traverse ground, young gentleman.

(FIDELIA *avoiding her*)

FIDELIA

I take breath only.

MANLY *(Aside)*

Good heavens! How was I deceived!

OLIVIA

Nay, you are a coward; what, are you afraid of the fierce-   190
ness of my love?

FIDELIA

Yes, madam, lest its violence might presage its change; and
I must needs be afraid you would leave me quickly, who
could desert so brave a gentleman as Manly.

OLIVIA

O, name not his name! For in a time of stolen joys, as this   195
is, the filthy name of husband were not a more allaying
sound.

MANLY *(Aside)*

There's some comfort yet.

FIDELIA

But did you not love him?

OLIVIA

Never. How could you think it?   200

FIDELIA

Because he thought it, who is a man of that sense, nice
discerning, and diffidency, that I should think it hard to
deceive him.

OLIVIA

No; he that distrusts most the world trusts most to himself,
and is but the more easily deceived because he thinks he can't   205
be deceived. His cunning is like the coward's sword, by which
he is oftener worsted than defended.

FIDELIA

Yet, sure, you used no common art to deceive him.

OLIVIA

I knew he loved his own singular moroseness so well as to
dote upon any copy of it; wherefore I feigned an hatred to   210
the world too, that he might love me in earnest. But if it had
been hard to deceive him, I'm sure 'twere much harder to

187 *traverse ground* move from side to side (like a fencer or pugilist)

love him. A dogged, ill-mannered—

FIDELIA *(Aside, to* MANLY*)*

D'ye hear her, sir? Pray hear her.

OLIVIA

Surly, untractable, snarling brute! He! A masty dog were as   215
fit a thing to make a gallant of.

MANLY *(Aside)*

Ay, a goat or monkey were fitter for thee.

FIDELIA

I must confess, for my part, though my rival, I cannot but
say he has a manly handsomeness in's face and mien.

OLIVIA

So has a Saracen in the sign.   220

FIDELIA

Is proper, and well made.

OLIVIA

As a drayman.

FIDELIA

Has wit.

OLIVIA

He rails at all mankind.

FIDELIA

And undoubted courage.   225

OLIVIA

Like the hangman's, can murder a man when his hands are
tied. He has cruelty indeed, which is no more courage than
his railing is wit.

MANLY *(Aside)*

Thus women, and men like women, are too hard for us when
they think we do not hear 'em; and reputation, like other   230
mistresses, is never true to a man in his absence.

FIDELIA

He is—

OLIVIA

Prithee, no more of him. I thought I had satisfied you
enough before that he could never be a rival for you to
apprehend, and you need not be more assured of my aversion   235

---

215 *masty dog* mastiff
220 *a Saracen in the sign* 'When our Country-men came home from
fighting with the *Saracens,* and were beaten by them, they pictured
them with huge, big, terrible Faces (as you still see the Sign of
the *Saracen*'s-head is)' (John Selden, *Table-Talk* (1689), p. 58); there
was a coaching inn of this name at Snow Hill, Newgate
221 *proper* handsome

to him but by the last testimony of my love to you, which I
am ready to give you. Come, my soul, this way—

(Pulls FIDELIA)

FIDELIA

But, madam, what could make you dissemble love to him,
when 'twas so hard a thing for you, and flatter his love to
you?   240

OLIVIA

That which makes all the world flatter and dissemble: 'twas
his money. I had a real passion for that. Yet I loved not that
so well as for it to take him, for as soon as I had his money,
I hastened his departure; like a wife who, when she has made
the most of a dying husband's breath, pulls away the pillow. 245

MANLY *(Aside)*

Damned money! Its master's potent rival still, and like a
saucy pimp corrupts itself the mistress it procures for us.

OLIVIA

But I did not think with you, my life, to pass my time in
talking. Come hither, come; yet stay, till I have locked a
door in the other room that may chance to let us in some   250
interruption, which reciting poets or losing gamesters fear
not more than I at this time do.   *(Exit* OLIVIA)

FIDELIA

Well, I hope you are now satisfied, sir, and will be gone to
think of your revenge.

MANLY

No, I am not satisfied, and must stay to be revenged.   255

FIDELIA

How, sir? You'll use no violence to her, I hope, and forfeit
your own life to take away hers? That were no revenge.

MANLY

No no, you need not fear; my revenge shall only be upon her
honour, not her life.

FIDELIA

How, sir? Her honour? O heavens! Consider, sir. she has no   260
honour. D'ye call that revenge? Can you think of such a
thing? But reflect, sir, how she hates and loathes you.

MANLY

Yes, so much she hates me, that it would be a revenge

246 s.d. *(Aside)* Q6–7 *(omitted* Q1–5, 8, 0)
250 *may* Q2–8, 0 (might Q1)

244–5 *wife . . . pillow* cf. *Love in a Wood* (1671); 'she is as arrant a Jilt,
as ever pull'd pillow from under husband's head' (II. i)

sufficient to make her accessary to my pleasure, and then let
her know it.   265

FIDELIA

No, sir, no; to be revenged on her now, were to disappoint
her. Pray, sir, let us be gone.   *(Pulls* MANLY*)*

MANLY

Hold off. What, you are my rival then; and therefore you
shall stay and keep the door for me, whilst I go in for you.
But when I'm gone, if you dare to stir off from this very   270
board, or breathe the least murmuring accent, I'll cut her
throat first; and if you love her, you will not venture her life.
Nay, then I'll cut your throat too; and I know you love your
own life at least.

FIDELIA

But sir, good sir.   275

MANLY

Not a word more, lest I begin my revenge on her by killing
you.

FIDELIA

But are you sure 'tis revenge that makes you do this? How
can it be?

MANLY

Whist!   280

FIDELIA

'Tis a strange revenge indeed.

MANLY

If you make me stay, I shall keep my word and begin with
you. No more.   *(Exit* MANLY, *at the same door* OLIVIA *went)*

Manet FIDELIA

FIDELIA

O heavens, is there not punishment enough
In loving well, if you will have't a crime,   285
But you must add fresh torments daily to't,
And punish us like peevish rivals still
Because we fain would find a heaven here?
But did there never any love like me,
That, untried tortures, you must find me out?   290
Others, at worst, you force to kill themselves,
But I must be self-murd'ress of my love,
Yet will not grant me power to end my life,

269 *go in for you* perhaps with a sexual *double entendre*
287 *peevish* foolish (?)

My cruel life; for when a lover's hopes
Are dead and gone, life is unmerciful.　　　　　　　　　　295

(Sits down and weeps)

Enter MANLY *to her*

MANLY

[*Aside*] I have thought better on't. I must not discover myself
now; I am without witnesses. For if I barely should publish
it, she would deny it with as much impudence as she would
act it again with this young fellow here. [*Aloud*] Where are
you?　　　　　　　　　　300

FIDELIA

Here. O—now I suppose we may be gone.

MANLY

I will, but not you. You must stay and act the second part
of a lover; that is, talk kindness to her.

FIDELIA

Not I, sir.

MANLY

No disputing, sir, you must; 'tis necessary to my design of　　305
coming again tomorrow night.

FIDELIA

What, can you come again then hither?

MANLY

Yes, and you must make the appointment, and an apology
for your leaving her so soon; for I have said not a word to
her, but have kept your counsel, as I expect you should do　　310
mine. Do this faithfully, and I promise you here, you shall
run my fortune still and we will never part as long as we
live; but if you do not do it, expect not to live.

FIDELIA

'Tis hard, sir, but such a consideration will make it easier.
You won't forget your promise, sir?　　　　　　　　315

MANLY

No, by heavens. But I hear her coming.　　　　*(Exit)*

Enter OLIVIA *to* FIDELIA

---

295 s.d. *Enter* MANLY During Fidelia's soliloquy he has lain with Olivia
　　but not revealed his identity.
297 *barely* baldly, without corroboration
310 *counsel* secret
312 *run my fortune still* share my lot always

OLIVIA

Where is my life? Run from me already! You do not love me, dearest; nay, you are angry with me, for you would not so much as speak a kind word to me within. What was the reason? 320

FIDELIA

I was transported too much.

OLIVIA

That's kind; but come, my soul, what make you here? Let us go in again; we may be surprised in this room, 'tis so near the stairs.

FIDELIA

No, we shall hear the better here, if anybody should come 325 up.

OLIVIA

Nay, I assure you, we shall be secure enough within. Come, come—

FIDELIA

I am sick, and troubled with a sudden dizziness; cannot stir yet. 330

OLIVIA

Come, I have spirits within.

FIDELIA

O!—Don't you hear a noise, madam?

OLIVIA

No no, there is none. Come, come.   *(Pulls her)*

FIDELIA

Indeed there is; and I love you so much I must have a care of your honour, if you won't, and go, but to come to you 335 tomorrow night, if you please.

OLIVIA

With all my soul. But you must not go yet. Come, prithee.

FIDELIA

O!—I am now sicker, and am afraid of one of my fits.

OLIVIA

What fits?

FIDELIA

Of the falling sickness; and I lie generally an hour in a 340 trance. Therefore pray consider your honour for the sake of my love, and let me go that I may return to you often.

OLIVIA

But will you be sure, then, to come tomorrow night?

340 *the falling sickness* epilepsy

FIDELIA

Yes.

OLIVIA

Swear.   345

FIDELIA

By our past kindness.

OLIVIA

Well, go your ways then, if you will, you naughty creature
you.   *(Exit* FIDELIA*)*
These young lovers, with their fears and modesty, make
themselves as bad as old ones to us; and I apprehend their   350
bashfulness more than their tattling.

FIDELIA returns

FIDELIA

O madam, we're undone! There was a gentleman upon the
stairs, coming up with a candle, which made me retire. Look
you, here he comes!

Enter VERNISH and his MAN with a light

OLIVIA

How! My husband! O, undone indeed! This way.   *(Exit)*   355

VERNISH

Ha! You shall not scape me so, sir.   *(Stops* FIDELIA*)*

FIDELIA *(Aside)*

O heavens, more fears, plagues, and torments yet in store!

VERNISH

Come, sir, I guess what your business was here, but this must
be your business now. Draw.   *(Draws)*

FIDELIA

Sir—   360

VERNISH

No expostulations; I shall not care to hear of't. Draw.

FIDELIA

Good sir!

VERNISH

How, you rascal! Not courage to draw, yet durst do me the
greatest injury in the world? Thy cowardice shall not save
thy life.   *(Offers to run at* FIDELIA*)*   365

FIDELIA

O hold, sir, and send but your servant down, and I'll satisfy
you, sir, I could not injure you as you imagine.

356 *scape* Q1 (escape Q2–8, 0)

VERNISH

Leave the light and be gone.   *(Exit* SERVANT*)*

Now quickly, sir, what you've to say, or—

FIDELIA

I am a woman, sir, a very unfortunate woman.   370

VERNISH

How! A very handsome woman, I'm sure then. *(Pulls off her peruke and feels her breasts)* Here are witnesses of't too, I confess. *(Aside)* Well, I'm glad to find the tables turned, my wife in more danger of cuckolding than I was.

FIDELIA

Now, sir, I hope you are so much a man of honour as to let   375 me go, now I have satisfied you, sir.

VERNISH

When you have satisfied me, madam, I will.

FIDELIA

I hope, sir, you are too much a gentleman to urge those secrets from a woman which concern her honour. You may guess my misfortune to be love by my disguise, but a pair of   380 breeches could not wrong you, sir.

VERNISH

I may believe love has changed your outside, which could not wrong me; but why did my wife run away?

FIDELIA

I know not, sir; perhaps because she would not be forced to discover me to you, or to guide me from your suspicions   385 that you might not discover me yourself; which ungentleman-like curiosity I hope you will cease to have, and let me go.

VERNISH

Well, madam, if I must not know who you are, 'twill suffice for me only to know certainly what you are, which you must not deny me. Come, there is a bed within, the proper rack   390 for lovers; and if you are a woman, there you can keep no secrets; you'll tell me there all unasked. Come.   *(Pulls her)*

FIDELIA

O! What d'ye mean? Help, O—

VERNISH

I'll show you; but 'tis in vain to cry out. No one dares help you, for I am lord here.   395

FIDELIA

Tyrant here! But if you are master of this house, which I have taken for a sanctuary, do not violate it yourself.

VERNISH

No, I'll preserve you here and nothing shall hurt you, and

will be as true to you as your disguise; but you must trust
me then. Come, come.   400

FIDELIA

O O! Rather than you shall drag me to a death so horrid
and so shameful, I'll die here a thousand deaths. But you do
not look like a ravisher, sir.

VERNISH

Nor you like one would put me to't, but if you will—

FIDELIA

O O! Help, help—   405

Enter SERVANT

VERNISH

You saucy rascal, how durst you come in when you heard
a woman squeak? That should have been your cue to shut
the door.

SERVANT

I come, sir, to let you know the alderman, coming home
immediately after you were at his house, has sent his cashier 410
with the money, according to your note.

VERNISH

Damn his money! Money never came to any, sure, unseason-
ably till now. Bid him stay.

SERVANT

He says he cannot a moment.

VERNISH

Receive it you, then.   415

SERVANT

He says he must have your receipt for it. He is in haste, for
I hear him coming up, sir.

VERNISH

Damn him. Help me in here then with this dishonourer of
my family.

FIDELIA

O! O!   420

SERVANT

You say she is a woman, sir.

VERNISH

No matter, sir. Must you prate?

FIDELIA

O heavens, is there— *(They thrust her in and lock the door)*

407 *shut* lock
422 *Must you prate?* probably addressed to Fidelia

VERNISH
    Stay there, my prisoner. You have a short reprieve.

            I'll fetch the gold, and that she can't resist;   425
            For with a full hand 'tis we ravish best.   *(Exeunt)*

                    Finis actus quarti

                    Act V, Scene i

                    ELIZA'*s Lodging*

                Enter OLIVIA *and* ELIZA

OLIVIA
    Ah, cousin, nothing troubles me but that I have given the
    malicious world its revenge and reason now, to talk as freely
    of me as I used to do of it.
ELIZA
    Faith, then, let not that trouble you; for to be plain, cousin,
    the world cannot talk worse of you than it did before.   5
OLIVIA
    How, cousin! I'd have you to know, before this *faux pas*,
    this trip of mine, the world could not talk of me.
ELIZA
    Only that you mind other people's actions so much that you
    take no care of your own, but to hide 'em; that, like a thief,
    because you know yourself most guilty, you impeach your   10
    fellow criminals first to clear yourself.
OLIVIA
    O wicked world!
ELIZA
    That you pretend an aversion to all mankind in public, only
    that their wives and mistresses may not be jealous, and
    hinder you of their conversation in private.   15
OLIVIA
    Base world!
ELIZA
    That abroad you fasten quarrels upon innocent men for
    talking of you, only to bring 'em to ask you pardon at home,
    and to become dear friends with 'em, who were hardly your
    acquaintance before.   20

19 *'em* Q1 (them Q2–8, O)

OLIVIA

Abominable world!

ELIZA

That you condemn the obscenity of modern plays, only that
you may not be censured for never missing the most obscene
of the old ones.

OLIVIA

Damned world!   25

ELIZA

That you deface the nudities of pictures and little statues
only because they are not real.

OLIVIA

O fie fie fie; hideous, hideous, cousin! The obscenity of their
censures makes me blush.

ELIZA

The truth of 'em, the naughty world would say now.   30

Enter LETTICE *hastily*

LETTICE

O madam, here is that gentleman coming up who now you
say is my master.

OLIVIA

O cousin, whither shall I run? Protect me, or—
                    (OLIVIA *runs away and stands at a distance*)

Enter VERNISH

VERNISH

Nay nay, come—

OLIVIA

O sir, forgive me.   35

VERNISH

Yes yes, I can forgive you being alone in the dark with a
woman in man's clothes; but have a care of a man in
woman's clothes.

OLIVIA *(Aside)*

What does he mean? He dissembles, only to get me into his
power. Or has my dear friend made him believe he was a   40
woman? My husband may be deceived by him, but I'm sure
I was not.

VERNISH

Come, come, you need not have lain out of your house for

26–7 borrowed from Célimène in Molière's *Le Misanthrope*: 'Elle fait
   des tableaux couvrir les nudités,/Mais elle a de l'amour pour les
   réalités' (943–4); Olivia echoes the same couplet at II. 452–4

this; but perhaps you were afraid, when I was warm with
suspicions, you must have discovered who she was; and 45
prithee, may I not know it?

OLIVIA

She was—*(Aside)* I hope he has been deceived; and since my
lover has played the card, I must not renounce.

VERNISH

Come, what's the matter with thee? If I must not know who
she is, I'm satisfied without. Come hither. 50

OLIVIA

Sure you do know her; she has told you herself, I suppose.

VERNISH

No; I might have known her better, but that I was interrupted by the goldsmith you know, and was forced to lock
her into your chamber to keep her from his sight; but when
I returned I found she was got away by tying the window 55
curtains to the balcony, by which she slid down into the
street. For, you must know, I jested with her and made her
believe I'd ravish her, which she apprehended, it seems, in
earnest.

OLIVIA

Then she got from you? 60

VERNISH

Yes.

OLIVIA

And is quite gone?

VERNISH

Yes.

OLIVIA

I'm glad on't—otherwise you had ravished her, sir? But how
dar'st you go so far as to make her believe you would ravish 65
her? Let me understand that, sir. What! There's guilt in your
face; you blush too; nay, then you did ravish her, you did,
you base fellow. What, ravish a woman in the first month of
our marriage! 'Tis a double injury to me, thou base, ungrateful man. Wrong my bed already, villain! I could tear out 70
those false eyes, barbarous, unworthy wretch.

ELIZA

So, so—

---

48 *renounce* fail to follow suit; in ombre, 'If you renounce you are to
double the Stake' (Charles Cotton, *The Compleat Gamester* (1674),
p. 102)
64 *I'm glad on't* perhaps an aside

VERNISH

Prithee hear, my dear.

OLIVIA

I will never hear you, my plague, my torment.

VERNISH

I swear—prithee, hear me.   75

OLIVIA

I have heard already too many of your false oaths and vows,
especially your last in the church. O wicked man! And
wretched woman that I was! I wish I had then sunk down
into a grave, rather than to have given you my hand, to be
led to your loathsome bed. O, O—   *(Seems to weep)*   80

VERNISH

So, very fine! Just a marriage quarrel! which, though it
generally begins by the wife's fault, yet in the conclusion it
becomes the husband's; and whosoever offends at first, he
only is sure to ask pardon at last. My dear—

OLIVIA

My devil!   85

VERNISH

Come, prithee be appeased and go home; I have bespoken
our supper betimes, for I could not eat till I found you. Go,
I'll give you all kind of satisfactions, and one which uses
to be a reconciling one: two hundred of those guineas I
received last night, to do what you will with.   90

OLIVIA

What, would you pay me for being your bawd?

VERNISH

Nay, prithee no more; go, and I'll thoroughly satisfy you
when I come home; and then, too, we will have a fit of
laughter at Manly, whom I am going to find at 'The Cock' in
Bow Street, where, I hear, he dined. Go, dearest, go home.   95

ELIZA *(Aside)*

A very pretty turn indeed, this!

VERNISH

Now, cousin, since by my wife I have that honour and
privilege of calling you so, I have something to beg of you

92 *thoroughly* Q1 (throughly Q2–8, 0)

---

81 *Just a marriage quarrel* A proper marriage quarrel
94–5 *'The Cock' in Bow Street* Oxford Kate's, a tavern notorious for
     Sedley's nude debauch (see Pepys, 1 July 1663); Wycherley enter-
     tained here when lodging in Bow Street

too; which is, not to take notice of our marriage to any
whatever yet awhile, for some reasons very important to me;   100
and next, that you will do my wife the honour to go home
with her, and me the favour to use that power you have
with her in our reconcilement.

ELIZA

That, I dare promise, sir, will be no hard matter. Your
servant.   (*Exit* VERNISH)   105
—Well, cousin, this I confess was reasonable hypocrisy; you
were the better for't.

OLIVIA

What hypocrisy?

ELIZA

Why, this last deceit of your husband was lawful, since in
your own defence.   110

OLIVIA

What deceit? I'd have you to know I never deceived my
husband.

ELIZA

You do not understand me, sure; I say, this was an honest
come-off, and a good one. But 'twas a sign your gallant had
had enough of your conversation, since he could so dex-   115
trously cheat your husband in passing for a woman.

OLIVIA

What d'ye mean, once more, with my gallant and passing for
a woman?

ELIZA

What do you mean? You see your husband took him for a
woman.   120

OLIVIA

Whom?

ELIZA

Heyday! Why, the man he found you with, for whom last
night you were so much afraid, and who you told me—

OLIVIA

Lord, you rave, sure!

ELIZA

Why, did not you tell me last night—   125

OLIVIA

I know not what I might tell you last night, in a fright.

99 *take notice of* mention
114 *come-off* evasion
115 *conversation* (1) society (2) sexual intimacy; Eliza suggests Olivia
has reduced her gallant to temporary impotence

ELIZA

Ay, what was that fright for? For a woman? Besides, were
you not afraid to see your husband just now? I warrant, only
for having been found with a woman! Nay, did you not just
now too own your false step, or trip, as you called it?   130
Which was with a woman too! Fie, this fooling is so insipid,
'tis offensive.

OLIVIA

And fooling with my honour will be more offensive. Did
you not hear my husband say he found me with a woman in
man's clothes? And d'ye think he does not know a man from   135
a woman?

ELIZA

Not so well, I'm sure, as you do; therefore I'd rather take
your word.

OLIVIA

What, you grow scurrilous and are, I find, more censorious
than the world! I must have a care of you, I see.   140

ELIZA

No, you need not fear yet; I'll keep your secret.

OLIVIA

My secret! I'd have you to know I have no need of confidents, though you value yourself upon being a good one.

ELIZA

O admirable confidence! You show more in denying your
wickedness than other people in glorying in't.   145

OLIVIA

Confidence, to me! To me, such language! Nay, then I'll
never see your face again. *(Aside)* I'll quarrel with her, that
people may never believe I was in her power, but take for
malice all the truth she may speak against me. [*Aloud*]
Lettice, where are you? Let us be gone from this censorious,   150
ill woman.

ELIZA

(Aside) Nay, thou shalt stay a little, to damn thyself quite.
[*Aloud*] One word first, pray, madam. Can you swear that
whom your husband found you with—

OLIVIA

Swear! Ay, that whosoever 'twas that stole up, unknown,   155
into my room when 'twas dark, I know not whether man or
woman, by heavens, by all that's good, or may I never more
have joys here or in the other world! Nay, may I eternally—

---

144 *confidence* impudence (with a pun on 'confidents')

ELIZA

Be damned. So so, you are damned enough already by your
oaths, and I enough confirmed; and now you may please to   160
be gone. Yet take this advice with you: in this plain-dealing
age, to leave off forswearing yourself. For when people
hardly think the better of a woman for her real modesty,
why should you put that great constraint upon yourself to
feign it?   165

OLIVIA

O hideous, hideous advice! Let us go out of the hearing of
it. She will spoil us, Lettice.

(Exeunt OLIVIA *and* LETTICE *at one door,* ELIZA *at t'other)*

[Act V, Scene ii]

The scene changes to 'The Cock' in Bow Street
A table, [*chair,*] *and bottles* [*set*]

MANLY *and* FIDELIA [*discovered*]

MANLY

How! Saved her honour by making her husband believe you
were a woman! 'Twas well, but hard enough to do, sure.

FIDELIA

We were interrupted before he could contradict me.

MANLY

But can't you tell me, d'ye say, what kind of man he was?

FIDELIA

I was so frightened, I confess, I can give no other account   5
of him but that he was pretty tall, round faced, and one I'm
sure I ne'er had seen before.

MANLY

But she, you say, made you swear to return tonight?

FIDELIA

But I have since sworn never to go near her again; for the
husband would murder me, or worse, if he caught me again.   10

MANLY

No, I'll go with you and defend you tonight, and then I'll
swear, too, never to go near her again.

FIDELIA

Nay, indeed, sir, I will not go, to be accessary to your death
too. Besides, what should you go again, sir, for?

167 *spoil* destroy, ruin

MANLY

No disputing or advice, sir; you have reason to know I am   15
unalterable. Go, therefore, presently, and write her a note to
enquire if her assignation with you holds, and if not to be at
her own house, where else; and be importunate to gain admittance to her tonight. Let your messenger, ere he deliver your
letter, enquire first if her husband be gone out. Go, 'tis now   20
almost six of the clock; I expect you back here before seven,
with leave to see her then. Go, do this dextrously, and expect
the performance of my last night's promise never to part with
you.

FIDELIA

Ay, sir, but will you be sure to remember that?   25

MANLY

Did I ever break my word? Go, no more replies or doubts.

(Exit FIDELIA*)*

Enter FREEMAN *to* MANLY

Where hast thou been?

FREEMAN

In the next room, with my Lord Plausible and Novel.

MANLY

Ay, we came hither because 'twas a private house, but with
thee indeed no house can be private, for thou hast that   30
pretty quality of the familiar fops of the town, who in an
eating-house always keep company with all people in't but
those they came with.

FREEMAN

I went into their room but to keep them, and my own fool
the squire, out of your room. But you shall be peevish now,   35
because you have no money. But why the devil won't you
write to those we were speaking of? Since your modesty, or
your spirit, will not suffer you to speak to 'em, to lend you
money, why won't you try 'em at last that way?

MANLY

Because I know 'em already, and can bear want better than   40
denials, nay, than obligations.

FREEMAN

Deny you! They cannot. All of 'em have been your intimate
friends.

MANLY

No, they have been people only I have obliged particularly.

29 *private house* inn with some rooms available for private parties

FREEMAN

Very well; therefore you ought to go to 'em the rather, sure.   45

MANLY

No no; those you have obliged most, most certainly avoid you when you can oblige 'em no longer; and they take your visits like so many duns. Friends, like mistresses, are avoided for obligations past.

FREEMAN

Pshaw! But most of 'em are your relations, men of great   50
fortune and honour.

MANLY

Yes, but relations have so much honour as to think poverty taints the blood, and disown their wanting kindred; believing, I suppose, that as riches at first makes a gentleman, the want of 'em degrades him. But, damn 'em, now I am poor I'll   55
anticipate their contempt and disown them.

FREEMAN

But you have many a female acquaintance whom you have been liberal to, who may have a heart to refund to you a little, if you would ask it. They are not all Olivias.

MANLY

Damn thee! How could'st thou think of such a thing? I   60
would as soon rob my footman of his wages. Besides, 'twere in vain too; for a wench is like a box in an ordinary, receives all people's money easily, but there's no getting, nay, shaking any out again, and he that fills it is surest never to keep the key.   65

FREEMAN

Well, but noble captain, would you make me believe that you who know half the town, have so many friends, and have obliged so many, can't borrow fifty or an hundred pound?

MANLY

Why, noble lieutenant, you who know all the town, and call   70
all you know friends, methinks should not wonder at it, since you find ingratitude too; for how many lords' families,

55 *I am* Q2–8, 0 (I'm Q1)
64 *surest* Q1b, 2–8 (sure Q1a, 0)

---

45 *the rather* sooner, more readily
62 *a box in an ordinary* i.e., the 'bank' at a public eating-house used for gambling: 'Rooks can do little harm in the day time at an *Ordinary,* being forc'd to play upon the *Square,* although now and then they make an advantage, when the *Box-keeper goes with* [them]' (Charles Cotton, *The Compleat Gamester* (1674), p. 5)

though descended from blacksmiths or tinkers, hast thou
called great and illustrious? how many ill tables called good
eating? how many noisy coxcombs wits? how many pert, 75
cocking cowards stout? how many tawdry, affected rogues
well-dressed? how many perukes admired? and how many
ill verses applauded? and yet canst not borrow a shilling.
Dost thou expect I, who always spoke truth, should?

FREEMAN

Nay, now you think you have paid me; but hark you, 80
captain, I have heard of a thing called grinning honour, but
never of starving honour.

MANLY

Well, but it has been the fate of some brave men; and if they
won't give me a ship again, I can go starve anywhere with
a musket on my shoulder. 85

FREEMAN

Give you a ship! Why, you will not solicit it.

MANLY

If I have not solicited it by my services, I know no other way.

FREEMAN

Your servant, sir. Nay, then I'm satisfied, I must solicit my
widow the closer, and run the desperate fortune of matrimony on shore. *(Exit)* 90

Enter to MANLY, VERNISH

MANLY

How! Nay, here is a friend indeed, and he that has him in
his arms can know no wants. *(Embraces* VERNISH*)*

VERNISH

Dear sir! And he that is in your arms is secure from all fears
whatever. Nay, our nation is secure by your defeat at sea,
and the Dutch that fought against you have proved enemies 95
to themselves only, in bringing you back to us.

---

74 *called good* Q6–7 (call good Q1–5, 8, 0)
76 *cocking* Q1b, 2–8 (coaching Q1a, 0)

---

76 *cocking* setting the hat with a flourish; hence, strutting, swaggering
76 *stout* brave
81 *grinning honour* Falstaff's comment on the dead Sir Walter Blunt in
1 Henry IV, V. iii, 59; Freeman suggests that Manly's integrity will
prove as fatal
88 *Your servant, sir* Freeman disagrees with Manly, and withdraws
from the discussion; see II. 271 note.
88 *satisfied* convinced
89 *run the desperate fortune* risk the dangerous undertaking

MANLY

Fie fie, this from a friend! And yet from any other 'twere unsufferable. I thought I should never have taken anything ill from you.

VERNISH

A friend's privilege is to speak his mind, though it be taken ill.   100

MANLY

But your tongue need not tell me you think too well of me; I have found it from your heart, which spoke in actions, your unalterable heart. But Olivia is false, my friend, which I suppose is no news to you.   105

VERNISH *(Aside)*

He's in the right on't.

MANLY

But could'st thou not keep her true to me?

VERNISH

Not for my heart, sir.

MANLY

But could you not perceive it at all before I went? Could she so deceive us both?   110

VERNISH

I must confess, the first time I knew it was three days after your departure, when she received the money you had left in Lombard Street in her name; and her tears did not hinder her, it seems, from counting that. You would trust her with all, like a true, generous lover!   115

MANLY

And she, like a mean, jilting—

VERNISH

Traitorous—

MANLY

Base—

VERNISH

Damned—

MANLY

Covetous—   120

VERNISH

Mercenary whore—*(Aside)* I can hardly hold from laughing.

---

113 *Lombard Street* in the heart of the city; many bankers traded here, including Pepys's Master Backwell (29 May 1662) who, like Vernish's associate in IV. ii, 155, 409, was also a goldsmith and an alderman

MANLY

Ay, a mercenary whore indeed, for she made me pay her
before I lay with her.

VERNISH

How!—Why, have you lain with her?

MANLY

Ay ay.   125

VERNISH

Nay, she deserves you should report it at least, though you
have not.

MANLY

Report it! By heaven, 'tis true.

VERNISH

How! Sure not.

MANLY

I do not use to lie, nor you to doubt me.   130

VERNISH

When?

MANLY

Last night, about seven or eight of the clock.

VERNISH

Ha! *(Aside)* Now I remember, I thought she spake as if she
expected some other, rather than me. A confounded whore
indeed!   135

MANLY

But what, thou wonderest at it! Nay, you seem to be angry
too.

VERNISH

I cannot but be enraged against her, for her usage of you.
Damned, infamous, common jade!

MANLY

Nay, her cuckold, who first cuckolded me in my money, shall 140
not laugh all himself; we will do him reason, shan't we?

VERNISH

Ay ay.

MANLY

But thou dost not, for so great a friend, take pleasure enough
in your friend's revenge, methinks.

VERNISH

Yes yes; I'm glad to know it, since you have lain with her. 145

MANLY

Thou canst not tell me who that rascal, her cuckold, is?

141 *do him reason* give him what he deserves

VERNISH

No.

MANLY

She would keep it from you, I suppose.

VERNISH

Yes, yes.

MANLY

Thou wouldst laugh if thou knewest but all the circum-   150
stances of my having her. Come, I'll tell thee.

VERNISH

Damn her! I care not to hear any more of her.

MANLY

Faith, thou shalt. You must know—

Enter FREEMAN *backwards, endeavouring to keep out* NOVEL,
LORD PLAUSIBLE, JERRY, *and* OLDFOX, *who all press in upon him*

FREEMAN

I tell you, he has a wench with him and would be private.

MANLY

Damn 'em! A man can't open a bottle in these eating-houses,   155
but presently you have these impudent, intruding, buzzing
flies and insects in your glass.—Well, I'll tell thee all anon.
In the mean time, prithee go to her, but not from me, and
try if you can get her to lend me but an hundred pound of
my money, to supply my present wants; for I suppose there   160
is no recovering any of it by law.

VERNISH

Not any; think not of it. Nor by this way neither.

MANLY

Go, try, at least.

VERNISH

I'll go, but I can satisfy you beforehand 'twill be to no
purpose. You'll no more find a refunding wench—   165

MANLY

Than a refunding lawyer; indeed their fees alike scarce ever
return. However, try her, put it to her.

VERNISH

Ay ay, I'll try her, put it to her home, with a vengeance.

(Exit VERNISH*)*

Manent caeteri

156 *presently* at once

NOVEL

Nay, you shall be our judge, Manly.—Come, major, I'll
speak it to your teeth. If people provoke me to say bitter 170
things to their faces, they must take what follows; though,
like my Lord Plausible, I'd rather do't civilly behind their
backs.

MANLY

Nay, thou art a dangerous rogue, I've heard, behind a man's
back. 175

LORD PLAUSIBLE

You wrong him sure, noble captain; he would do a man no
more harm behind his back than to his face.

FREEMAN

I am of my lord's mind.

MANLY

Yes, a fool, like a coward, is the more to be feared behind
a man's back, more than a witty man; for as a coward is 180
more bloody than a brave man, a fool is more malicious than
a man of wit.

NOVEL

A fool, tar, a fool! Nay, thou art a brave sea-judge of wit!
A fool! Prithee, when did you ever find me want something
to say, as you do often? 185

MANLY

Nay, I confess thou art always talking, roaring, or making a
noise; that I'll say for thee.

NOVEL

Well, and is talking a sign of a fool?

MANLY

Yes, always talking, especially too if it be loud and fast, is
the sign of a fool. 190

NOVEL

Pshaw! Talking is like fencing, the quicker the better; run
'em down, run 'em down, no matter for parrying, push on
still, sa, sa, sa! no matter whether you argue in form, push in
guard, or no.

MANLY

Or hit, or no. I think thou always talk'st without thinking, 195
Novel.

170 *to your teeth* face to face, in direct confrontation
186 *roaring* roistering, behaving riotously
192 *push on* press forward
193 *sa, sa, sa* a hunting cry, used here for a fencer's attacking advance
193–4 *push in guard* attack from a defensive position

G

NOVEL

Ay ay, studied play's the worse, to follow the allegory, as the
old pedant says.

OLDFOX

A young fop!

MANLY

I ever thought the man of most wit had been like him of   200
most money, who has no vanity in showing it everywhere,
whilst the beggarly pusher of his fortune has all he has about
him still, only to show.

NOVEL

Well, sir, and makes a very pretty show in the world, let me
tell you; nay, a better than your close hunks. A pox, give me   205
ready money in play. What care I for a man's reputation?
What are we the better for your substantial, thrifty cur-
mudgeon in wit, sir?

LORD PLAUSIBLE

Thou art a profuse young rogue, indeed.

NOVEL

So much for talking, which I think I have proved a mark of   210
wit; and so is railing, roaring, and making a noise, for railing
is satire, you know, and roaring and making a noise, humour.

Enter to them FIDELIA, *taking* MANLY *aside and showing him
a paper*

FIDELIA

The hour is betwixt seven and eight exactly. 'Tis now half an
hour after six.

MANLY

Well, go then to the Piazza and wait for me; as soon as it is   215
quite dark, I'll be with you. I must stay here yet awhile for
my friend.   *(Exit* FIDELIA*)*
But is railing satire, Novel?

197 *studied play* premeditated sword-play
197 *follow the allegory* continue the metaphor
198 *old pedant* unidentified
202 *pusher* promoter
205 *hunks* 'a covetous Creature, a miserable Wretch' (*B.E.*)
213 *betwixt . . . exactly* i.e., 'half an hour after seven precisely' (329)
215 *the Piazza* 'On the North and East Sides [of Covent Garden] are
Rows of very good and large Houses, called the *Piazzo's,* sustained
by Stone Pillars, to support the Buildings. Under which are Walks,
broad and convenient, paved with Freestone' (John Stow, *A survey of
. . . London,* ed. John Strype (1720), VI, 89)

FREEMAN

And roaring and making a noise, humour?

NOVEL

What, won't you confess there's humour in roaring and mak-   220
ing a noise?

FREEMAN

No.

NOVEL

Nor in cutting napkins and hangings?

MANLY

No, sure.

NOVEL

Dull fops!   225

OLDFOX

O rogue, rogue, insipid rogue!—Nay, gentlemen, allow him
those things for wit, for his parts lie only that way.

NOVEL

Peace, old fool! I wonder not at thee; but that young fellows
should be so dull as to say there's no humour in making a
noise and breaking windows! I tell you, there's wit and   230
humour too in both, and a wit is as well known by his frolic
as by his simile.

OLDFOX

Pure rogue! There's your modern wit for you! Wit and
humour in breaking of windows! There's mischief, if you
will, but no wit or humour.   235

NOVEL

Prithee, prithee, peace, old fool. I tell you, where there is
mischief there's wit. Don't we esteem the monkey a wit
amongst beasts, only because he's mischievous? And let me
tell you, as good nature is a sign of a fool, being mischievous
is a sign of wit.   240

OLDFOX

O rogue, rogue! Pretend to be a wit by doing mischief and
railing!

---

223 *cutting . . . hangings* putting a sword through the table linen and
curtains of an inn or whore's lodging

227 *parts* abilities, talents

230 *breaking windows* another pastime of the roaring boys; in
Etherege's *The Comical Revenge* (1664) Sir Frederick Frollick
'committed a general massacre on the glass-windows' of his whore's
lodging (I. ii); cf. 373–5

237 *monkey* a fashionable pet; Huysmans painted Rochester crowning
his with a laurel wreath

NOVEL

Why, thou, old fool, hast no other pretence to the name of
a wit but by railing at new plays.

OLDFOX

Thou, by railing at that facetious, noble way of wit, quib-   245
bling.

NOVEL

Thou call'st thy dullness gravity, and thy dozing thinking.

OLDFOX

You, sir, your dullness spleen; and you talk much and say
nothing.

NOVEL

Thou read'st much and understand'st nothing, sir.   250

OLDFOX

You laugh loud and break no jest.

NOVEL

You rail, and nobody hangs himself. And thou hast nothing
of the satyr but in thy face.

OLDFOX

And you have no jest but your face, sir.

NOVEL

Thou art an illiterate pedant.   255

OLDFOX

Thou art a fool with a bad memory.

MANLY

Come, a pox on you both! You have done like wits now; for
you wits, when you quarrel, never give over till you prove
one another fools.

NOVEL

And you fools have never any occasion of laughing at us   260
wits but when we quarrel.—Therefore, let us be friends,
Oldfox.

MANLY

They are such wits as thou art who make the name of a wit
as scandalous as that of bully, and signify a loud-laughing,

245–6 *quibbling* punning
248 *spleen* melancholy, a fashionable malady; 'every heavy wretch, who
     has nothing to say, excuses his dulness by complaining of the
     spleen' (the *Spectator* no. 53, 1 May 1711)
253 *satyr* Satire was thought to derive from the chorus of lustful goat-
     like satyrs in Greek drama; thus Novel attacks simultaneously Old-
     fox's virility, appearance, and wit.

talking, incorrigible coxcomb, as bully a roaring, hardened　265
coward.

FREEMAN

And would have his noise and laughter pass for wit, as
t'other his huffing and blustering for courage.

Enter VERNISH

MANLY

Gentlemen, with your leave, here is one I would speak with,
and I have nothing to say to you. *(Puts 'em out of the room)*　270

Manent MANLY, VERNISH

VERNISH

I told you 'twas in vain to think of getting money out of her.
She says, if a shilling would do't, she would not save you
from starving or hanging or, what you would think worse,
begging or flattering; and rails so at you, one would not
think you had lain with her.　275

MANLY

O friend, never trust for that matter a woman's railing, for
she is no less a dissembler in her hatred than her love; and
as her fondness of her husband is a sign he's a cuckold, her
railing at another man is a sign she lies with him.

VERNISH *(Aside)*

He's in the right on't; I know not what to trust to.　280

MANLY

But you did not take any notice of it to her, I hope?

VERNISH *(Aside)*

So! Sure he is afraid I should have disproved him by an
enquiry of her; all may be well yet.

MANLY

What hast thou in thy head that makes thee seem so unquiet?

VERNISH

Only this base, impudent woman's falseness; I cannot put her　285
out of my head.

MANLY

O my dear friend, be not you too sensible of my wrongs, for
then I shall feel 'em too with more pain, and think 'em
unsufferable. Damn her, her money, and that ill-natured

---

265 *hardened* confirmed
268 *huffing* swaggering
281 *take any notice of* mention

whore too, Fortune herself! But if thou would'st ease a little   290
my present trouble, prithee go borrow me somewhere else
some money; I can trouble thee.

VERNISH

You trouble me indeed, most sensibly, when you command
me anything I cannot do. I have lately lost a great deal of
money at play, more than I can yet pay, so that not only my   295
money but my credit too is gone, and know not where to
borrow; but could rob a church for you. *(Aside)* Yet would
rather end your wants by cutting your throat.

MANLY

Nay, then I doubly feel my poverty, since I'm incapable of
supplying thee.   *(Embraces* VERNISH*)*   300

VERNISH

But, methinks, she that granted you the last favour, as they
call it, should not deny you anything.

NOVEL *looks in*

NOVEL

Hey, tarpaulin, have you done?   *(*[NOVEL] *retires again)*

VERNISH

I understand not that point of kindness, I confess.

MANLY

No, thou dost not understand it, and I have not time to let   305
you know all now, for these fools, you see, will interrupt us;
but anon, at supper, we'll laugh at leisure together at Olivia's
cuckold, who took a young fellow, that goes between his wife
and me, for a woman.

VERNISH

Ha!   310

MANLY

Senseless, easy rascal! 'Twas no wonder she chose him for a
husband; but she thought him, I thank her, fitter than me for
that blind, bearing office.

VERNISH *(Aside)*

I could not be deceived in that long woman's hair tied up
behind, nor those infallible proofs, her pouting, swelling   315
breasts; I have handled too many, sure, not to know 'em.

---

303 s.d. After 'done' Q1 prints (NOVEL *looks in, and retires again*).

292-3 *trouble* (1) inconvenience (2) distress; Manly uses the formula of
     a polite request, which Vernish takes up seriously
313 *bearing* suffering, enduring

MANLY

What, you wonder the fellow could be such a blind coxcomb?

VERNISH

Yes, yes—

NOVEL *looks in again*

NOVEL

Nay, prithee come to us, Manly. Gad, all the fine things one   320
says in their company are lost without thee.

MANLY

Away, fop! I'm busy yet.   *(*[NOVEL] *retires)*
You see we cannot talk here at our ease; besides, I must be
gone immediately, in order to meeting with Olivia again
tonight.   325

VERNISH

Tonight! It cannot be, sure—

MANLY

I had an appointment just now from her.

VERNISH

For what time?

MANLY

At half an hour after seven precisely.

VERNISH

Don't you apprehend the husband?   330

MANLY

He! Snivelling gull! He a thing to be feared! A husband, the
tamest of creatures!

VERNISH *(Aside)*

Very fine!

MANLY

But, prithee, in the mean time, go try to get me some money.
Though thou art too modest to borrow for thyself, thou   335
canst do anything for me, I know. Go, for I must be gone
to Olivia. Go, and meet me here anon.—Freeman, where are
you?   *(Exit* MANLY*)*

Manet VERNISH

VERNISH

Ay, I'll meet with you, I warrant, but it shall be at Olivia's.
Sure, it cannot be; she denies it so calmly, and with that   340

---

319 s.d. After 'yes—' Q1 prints (NOVEL *looks in again, and retires*).

324 *in order to* for the sake of

honest, modest assurance, it can't be true—and he does not
use to lie—but belying a woman when she won't be kind is
the only lie a brave man will least scruple. But then the
woman in man's clothes, whom he calls a man! Well, but by
her breasts I know her to be a woman. But then again, his   345
appointment from her to meet with him tonight! I am dis-
tracted more with doubt than jealousy. Well, I have no
way to disabuse or revenge myself but by going home
immediately, putting on a riding suit, and pretending to my
wife the same business which carried me out of town last   350
requires me again to go post to Oxford tonight. Then, if the
appointment he boasts of be true, it's sure to hold, and I shall
have an opportunity either of clearing her or revenging
myself on both. Perhaps she is his wench of an old date,
and I am his cully, whilst I think him mine, and he has   355
seemed to make his wench rich only that I might take her
off his hands; or if he has but lately lain with her, he must
needs discover by her my treachery to him, which I'm sure
he will revenge with my death, and which I must prevent
with his, if it were only but for fear of his too just   360
reproaches; for I must confess I never had till now any
excuse but that of interest for doing ill to him.

(Exit VERNISH*)*

Re-enter MANLY *and* FREEMAN

MANLY

Come hither; only, I say, be sure you mistake not the time.
You know the house exactly where Olivia lodges; 'tis just
hard by.   365

FREEMAN

Yes yes.

MANLY

Well then, bring 'em all, I say, thither, and all you know
that may be then in the house; for the more witnesses I have
of her infamy, the greater will be my revenge. And be sure
you come straight up to her chamber, without more ado.   370
Here, take the watch. You see 'tis above a quarter past
seven. Be there in half an hour exactly.

FREEMAN

You need not doubt my diligence or dexterity; I am an old

357 *off* Q2–8, 0 (off of Q1)

351 *post* by post-horses, i.e., speedily
371 *above* after

scourer, and can naturally beat up a wench's quarters that
won't be civil. Shan't we break her windows too?   375
MANLY

No no. Be punctual only.   *(Exeunt ambo)*

Enter WIDOW BLACKACRE *and two* KNIGHTS OF THE POST, *a*
WAITER *with wine*

WIDOW

Sweetheart, are you sure the door was shut close, that none
of those roisters saw us come in?

WAITER

Yes, mistress; and you shall have a privater room above
instantly.   *(Exit* WAITER*)*   380

WIDOW

You are safe enough, gentlemen, for I have been private in
this house ere now upon other occasions, when I was something younger. Come, gentlemen; in short, I leave my business
to your care and fidelity; and so, here's to you.

1 KNIGHT

We were ungrateful rogues if we should not be honest to   385
you, for we have had a great deal of your money.

WIDOW

And you have done me many a good job for't; and so, here's
to you again.

2 KNIGHT

Why, we have been perjured but six times for you.

1 KNIGHT

Forged but four deeds, with your husband's last deed of gift.   390

2 KNIGHT

And but three wills.

1 KNIGHT

And counterfeited hands and seals to some six bonds; I
think that's all, brother.

WIDOW

Ay, that's all, gentlemen; and so, here's to you again.

2 KNIGHT

Nay, 'twould do one's heart good to be forsworn for you;   395
you have a conscience in your ways, and pay us well.

1 KNIGHT

You are in the right on't, brother; one would be damned for
her with all one's heart.

374 *scourer* roisterer
374 *beat . . . quarters* raid a whore's lodging

H

2 KNIGHT

But there are rogues who make us forsworn for 'em, and when we come to be paid, they'll be forsworn too, and not 400 pay us our wages, which they promised with oaths sufficient.

1 KNIGHT

Ay, a great lawyer that shall be nameless bilked me too.

WIDOW

That was hard, methinks, that a lawyer should use gentlemen witnesses no better.

2 KNIGHT

A lawyer! D'ye wonder a lawyer should do't? I was bilked 405 by a reverend divine, that preaches twice on Sundays and prays half an hour still before dinner.

WIDOW

How! A conscientious divine, and not pay people for damning themselves! Sure then, for all his talking, he does not believe damnation. But come, to our business. Pray be sure 410 to imitate exactly the flourish at the end of this name.

(Pulls out a deed or two)

1 KNIGHT

O he's the best in England at untangling a flourish, madam.

WIDOW

And let not the seal be a jot bigger. Observe well the dash too, at the end of this name.

2 KNIGHT

I warrant you, madam. 415

WIDOW

Well, these and many other shifts poor widows are put to sometimes; for everybody would be riding a widow, as they say, and breaking into her jointure. They think marrying a widow an easy business, like leaping the hedge where another has gone over before; a widow is a mere gap, a gap with 420 them.

Enter to them MAJOR OLDFOX *with two* WAITERS. *The* KNIGHTS OF THE POST *huddle up the writings*

What, he here! Go then, go, my hearts, you have your instructions. *(Exeunt* KNIGHTS OF THE POST*)*

OLDFOX

Come, madam, to be plain with you, I'll be fobbed off no longer. *(Aside)* I'll bind her and gag her, but she shall hear 425

402 *bilked* cheated
421 s.d. *huddle up* hide (in a heap)

me. [*To the* WAITERS] Look you, friends, there's the money
I promised you; and now do what you promised me. Here
are my garters, and here's a gag. [*To* WIDOW BLACKACRE]
You shall be acquainted with my parts, lady, you shall.
WIDOW

Acquainted with your parts! A rape, a rape! What, will you   430
ravish me?

    (The WAITERS *tie her to the chair and gag her, and exeunt)*
OLDFOX

Yes, lady, I will ravish you; but it shall be through the ear,
lady, the ear only, with my well-penned acrostics.

Enter to them FREEMAN, JERRY BLACKACRE, *three* BAILIFFS, *a*
CONSTABLE *and his* ASSISTANTS, *with the two* KNIGHTS OF THE
POST [*as prisoners*]

What, shall I never read my things undisturbed again?
JERRY

O law! My mother bound hand and foot, and gaping as if   435
she rose before her time today!

FREEMAN

What means this, Oldfox? [*To* WIDOW BLACKACRE] But I'll
release you from him; you shall be no man's prisoner but
mine.—Bailiffs, execute your writ.   *(*FREEMAN *unties her)*
OLDFOX [*Aside*]

Nay, then I'll be gone, for fear of being bail and paying her   440
debts without being her husband.   *(Exit* OLDFOX*)*
1 BAILIFF [*To* WIDOW BLACKACRE]

We arrest you in the King's name at the suit of Master
Freeman, guardian to Jeremiah Blackacre, esquire, in an
action of ten thousand pounds.

WIDOW

How! How! In a choke-bail action! What, and the pen and   445
ink gentlemen taken too!—Have you confessed, you rogues?
1 KNIGHT

We needed not to confess, for the bailiffs dogged us hither
to the very door and overheard all that you and we said.
WIDOW

Undone, undone then! No man was ever too hard for me till

428 *garters* long ribbons worn at the knee for display: 'I was set upon
    by a great dogg, who got hold of my garters' (Pepys, 11 May 1663)
429 *parts* abilities, talents, which the Widow takes in a sexual sense
435 *gaping* staring wildly
445 *choke-bail action* one where such large sums or serious offences are
    involved that bail is not allowed

now.—O Jerry, child, wilt thou vex again the womb that bore   450
thee?

JERRY

Ay, for bearing me before wedlock, as you say. But I'll teach
you to call a Blackacre a bastard, though you were never so
much my mother.

WIDOW

(Aside) Well, I'm undone. Not one trick left? No law-meuse   455
imaginable? [*To* FREEMAN] Cruel sir, a word with you, I pray.

FREEMAN

In vain, madam; for you have no other way to release yourself but by the bonds of matrimony.

WIDOW

How, sir, how! That were but to sue out an *habeas corpus*
for a removal from one prison to another. Matrimony!   460

FREEMAN

Well, bailiffs, away with her.

WIDOW

O stay, sir; can you be so cruel as to bring me under covert-
baron again, and put it out of my power to sue in my own
name? Matrimony to a woman is worse than excommunica-
tion, in depriving her of the benefit of the law, and I would   465
rather be deprived of life. But hark you, sir; I am contented
you should hold and enjoy my person by lease or patent, but
not by the spiritual patent called a licence; that is, to have
the privileges of a husband without the dominion; that is,
durante beneplacito: in consideration of which I will, out of   470
my jointure, secure you an annuity of three hundred pounds
a year and pay your debts; and that's all you younger
brothers desire to marry a widow for, I'm sure.

FREEMAN

Well, widow, if—

JERRY

What! I hope, bully guardian, you are not making agree-   475
ments without me?

464 *woman is* Q4–8, 0 (woman, Q1–3)

---

455 *law-meuse* loophole in the law
462–3 *under covert-baron* see II. 951 note; wives 'are wholly . . . at the
       Will and Disposition of the Husband . . . The Wife can make no
       Contract without her Husbands consent, and in Law-Matters *Sine
       viro respondere non potest*' (Chamberlayne, I, 291)
470 *durante beneplacito* during good pleasure, i.e., as long as one pleases;
       a legal phrase more usually applied to the tenure of judges in e.g.
       the Common Pleas.

FREEMAN

No no. First, widow, you must say no more that he is the son of a whore; have a care of that. And then he must have a settled exhibition of forty pounds a year, and a nag of assizes, kept by you, but not upon the common; and have 480 free ingress, egress, and regress to and from your maids' garret.

WIDOW

Well, I can grant all that too.

JERRY

Ay ay, fair words butter no cabbage; but, guardian, make her sign, sign and seal; for otherwise, if you knew her as well 485 as I, you would not trust her word for a farthing.

FREEMAN

I warrant thee, squire.—Well, widow, since thou art so generous, I will be generous too; and if you'll secure me four hundred pound a year but during your life, and pay my debts, not above a thousand pound, I'll bate you your person 490 to dispose of as you please.

WIDOW

Have a care, sir; a settlement without a consideration is void in the law. You must do something for't.

FREEMAN

Prithee, then let the settlement on me be called alimony, and the consideration our separation. Come; my lawyer, with 495 writings ready drawn, is within, and in haste. Come.

WIDOW

But what, no other kind of consideration, Master Freeman? Well, a widow, I see, is a kind of a *sine cure*, by custom of which the unconscionable incumbent enjoys the profits without any duty, but does that still elsewhere. *(Exeunt omnes)* 500

493 *in the* Q2–8 (in Q1, 0)

---

479 *settled exhibition* fixed allowance
479–80 *of assizes* of guaranteed quality
480 *not upon the common* since the grass is greener in a private field than in pastures available to all
481 *ingress . . . regress* entry, exit, and re-entry (legal terms)
484 *fair . . . cabbage* cf. 'Fair words butter no parsnips' (M. P. Tilley, *A Dictionary of the Proverbs in England in the Sixteenth and Seventeenth Centuries* (Ann Arbor, 1950), W791)
490 *bate you your person* i.e., make no sexual demands on you
496 *in haste* so is Freeman, who promised Manly at 373 to be at Olivia's with a gang of witnesses in half an hour

[Act V, Scene iii]

The scene changes to OLIVIA's *Lodging*
Enter OLIVIA *with a candle in her hand*

OLIVIA

So, I am now prepared once more for my timorous young
lover's reception. My husband is gone; and go thou out too,
thou next interrupter of love. *(Puts out the candle)* Kind
darkness, that frees us lovers from scandal and bashfulness,
from the censure of our gallants and the world! So, are you   5
there?

Enter to OLIVIA, FIDELIA, *followed softly by* MANLY

Come, my dear punctual lover; there is not such another in
the world. Thou hast beauty and youth to please a wife,
address and wit to amuse and fool a husband; nay, thou
hast all things to be wished in a lover, but your fits. I hope,   10
my dear, you won't have one tonight; and that you may not,
I'll lock the door, though there be no need of it but to lock
out your fits, for my husband is just gone out of town again.
Come, where are you?   *(Goes to the door and locks it)*

MANLY *(Aside)*

Well, thou hast impudence enough to give me fits too and   15
make revenge itself impotent, hinder me from making thee
yet more infamous, if it can be.

OLIVIA

Come, come, my soul, come.

FIDELIA

Presently, my dear; we have time enough, sure.

OLIVIA

How! Time enough! True lovers can no more think they   20
ever have time enough than love enough. You shall stay with
me all night; but that is but a lover's moment. Come.

FIDELIA

But won't you let me give you and myself the satisfaction of
telling you how I abused your husband last night?

OLIVIA

Not when you can give me and yourself too the satisfaction   25
of abusing him again tonight. Come.

9 *amuse* deceive

FIDELIA

Let me but tell you how your husband—

OLIVIA

O name not his or Manly's more loathsome name, if you
love me! I forbid 'em last night; and you know I mentioned
my husband but once, and he came. No talking, pray; 'twas   30
ominous to us. *(A noise at the door)* You make me fancy a
noise at the door already, but I'm resolved not to be interrupted. Where are you? Come; for rather than lose my dear
expectation now, though my husband were at the door, and
the bloody ruffian Manly here in the room with all his awful   35
insolence, I would give myself to this dear hand, to be led
away to heavens of joys which none but thou canst give.
(The noise at the door increases) But what's this noise at the
door? So, I told you what talking would come to. Ha!
(OLIVIA listens at the door) O heavens, my husband's voice!   40

MANLY *(Aside)*

Freeman is come too soon.

OLIVIA

O 'tis he! Then here's the happiest minute lost that ever
bashful boy or trifling woman fooled away! I'm undone! My
husband's reconcilement too was false as my joy, all delusion.
But come this way; here's a back door.   *(Exit, and returns)*   45
The officious jade has locked us in, instead of locking others
out. But let us then escape your way, by the balcony; and
whilst you pull down the curtains I'll fetch from my closet
what next will best secure our escape. I have left my key in
the door, and 'twill not suddenly be broke open.   *(Exit)*   50
                    (A noise as it were people forcing the door)

MANLY

Stir not; yet fear nothing.

FIDELIA

Nothing but your life, sir.

MANLY

We shall now know this happy man she calls husband.

OLIVIA re-enters

OLIVIA

O, where are you? What, idle with fear? Come, I'll tie the
curtains, if you will hold. Here, take this cabinet and purse,   55
for it is thine if we escape. *(MANLY takes from her the cabinet
and purse)* Therefore let us make haste.   *(Exit OLIVIA)*

42 *here's* Q2–6, 8, 0 (here is Q1; her's Q7)

MANLY

'Tis mine indeed now again, and it shall never escape more
from me, to you at least.

The door broken open, enter VERNISH *alone, with a dark-
lantern and a sword, running at* MANLY, *who draws, puts by the
thrust and defends himself, whilst* FIDELIA *runs at* VERNISH
behind

VERNISH *(With a low voice)*

So, there I'm right, sure—   60

MANLY *(Softly)*

Sword and dark-lantern, villain, are some odds, but—

VERNISH *(With a low voice)*

Odds! I'm sure I find more odds than I expected. What, has
my insatiable two seconds at once? But—

Whilst they fight, OLIVIA *re-enters, tying two curtains together*

OLIVIA

Where are you now?—What, is he entered then, and are they
fighting?—O do not kill one that can make no defence!   65
(MANLY *throws* VERNISH *down and disarms him)* How! But
I think he has the better on't. Here's his scarf; 'tis he.—So,
keep him down still. I hope thou hast no hurt, my dearest?
                                        (Embracing MANLY)

Enter to them FREEMAN, LORD PLAUSIBLE, NOVEL, JERRY
BLACKACRE, *and the* WIDOW BLACKACRE, *lighted in by the
two* SAILORS *with torches*

Ha! What? Manly!—And have I been thus concerned for
him, embracing him? And has he his jewels again too? What   70
means this? O 'tis too sure, as well as my shame, which I'll
go hide for ever.   *(Offers to go out;* MANLY *stops her)*

MANLY

No, my dearest; after so much kindness as has passed
between us, I cannot part with you yet.—Freeman, let
nobody stir out of the room; for notwithstanding your lights,   75

---

59 s.d. *dark-lantern* one shuttered to direct the light, thus blinding an
    onlooker
67 *his scarf* Perhaps Olivia kneels to identify Vernish by his sash; if
    she feels Manly's, it must resemble one usually worn by Fidelia (see
    II. 613 note).
72 s.d. *Offers* Attempts

we are yet in the dark till this gentleman please to turn his
face. *(Pulls* VERNISH *by the sleeve)* How! Vernish! Art thou
the happy man then? Thou! Thou! Speak, I say; but thy
guilty silence tells me all. Well, I shall not upbraid thee, for
my wonder is striking me as dumb as thy shame has made   80
thee.—But, what? My little volunteer, hurt and fainting!

FIDELIA

My wound, sir, is but a slight one in my arm; 'tis only my
fear of your danger, sir, not yet well over.

MANLY

But what's here? More strange things! *(Observing* FIDELIA's
*hair untied behind, and without a peruke, which she lost in
the scuffle)* What means this long woman's hair? and face,   85
now all of it appears, too beautiful for a man, which I still
thought womanish indeed! What, you have not deceived me
too, my little volunteer?

OLIVIA *(Aside)*

Me she has, I'm sure.

MANLY

Speak.   90

Enter ELIZA *and* LETTICE

ELIZA

What, cousin, I am brought hither by your woman, I suppose,
to be a witness of the second vindication of your honour?

OLIVIA

Insulting is not generous. You might spare me; I have you.

ELIZA

Have a care, cousin. You'll confess anon too much, and I
would not have your secrets.   95

MANLY *(To* FIDELIA*)*

Come, your blushes answer me sufficiently, and you have
been my volunteer in love.

FIDELIA

I must confess I needed no compulsion to follow you all the
world over, which I attempted in this habit, partly out of
shame to own my love to you, and fear of a greater shame,   100
your refusal of it; for I knew of your engagement to this
lady, and the constancy of your nature, which nothing could
have altered but herself.

MANLY

Dear madam, I desired you to bring me out of confusion,
and you have given me more. I know not what to speak to   105
you, or how to look upon you. The sense of my rough, hard,

and ill usage of you, though chiefly your own fault, gives me
more pain now 'tis over than you had when you suffered it;
and if my heart, the refusal of such a woman *(Pointing to*
OLIVIA*)*, were not a sacrifice to profane your love, and a   110
greater wrong to you than ever yet I did you, I would beg
of you to receive it, though you used it as she had done; for
though it deserved not from her the treatment she gave it, it
does from you.

FIDELIA

Then it has had punishment sufficient from her already, and   115
needs no more from me; and, I must confess, I would not be
the only cause of making you break your last night's oath to
me, of never parting with me, if you do not forget or
repent it.

MANLY

Then take for ever my heart, and this with it *(Gives her the*   120
cabinet), for 'twas given to you before, and my heart was
before your due. I only beg leave to dispose of these few.
—Here, madam, I never yet left my wench unpaid.

(Takes some of the jewels and offers 'em to OLIVIA; *she*
strikes 'em down; PLAUSIBLE *and* NOVEL *take 'em up)*

OLIVIA

So it seems, by giving her the cabinet.

LORD PLAUSIBLE

These pendants appertain to your most faithful, humble   125
servant.

NOVEL

And this locket is mine; my earnest for love, which she never
paid, therefore my own again.

WIDOW

By what law, sir, pray?—Cousin Olivia, a word. What, do
they make a seizure on your goods and chattels, *vi et armis*?   130
Make your demand, I say, and bring your trover, bring your
trover. I'll follow the law for you.

OLIVIA

And I my revenge.   *(Exit* OLIVIA*)*

MANLY

(To VERNISH*)* But 'tis, my friend, in your consideration most
that I would have returned part of your wife's portion, for   135

127 *earnest* initial payment (cf. 'earnest pence' IV. ii, 64 note)
130 *vi et armis* with force and weapons, i.e., by force of arms; a legal
     phrase often used in complaints of assault
131 *trover* strictly, 'an action against him who having found another
     mans goods, refuseth to deliver them upon demand' (Phillips)

'twere hard to take all from thee, since thou hast paid so
dear for't in being such a rascal. Yet thy wife is a fortune
without a portion, and thou art a man of that extraordinary
merit in villainy the world and fortune can never desert thee,
though I do; therefore be not melancholy. Fare you well, 140
sir. *(Exit* VERNISH *doggedly)*
Now, madam *(Turning to* FIDELIA*)*, I beg your pardon for
lessening the present I made you; but my heart can never be
lessened. This, I confess, was too small for you before, for
you deserve the Indian world, and I would now go thither 145
out of covetousness for your sake only.

FIDELIA

Your heart, sir, is a present of that value I can never make
any return to't. *(Pulling* MANLY *from the company)* But I can
give you back such a present as this, which I got by the loss
of my father, a gentleman of the north of no mean extrac- 150
tion, whose only child I was; therefore left me in the present
possession of two thousand pounds a year, which I left, with
multitudes of pretenders, to follow you, sir, having in several
public places seen you, and observed your actions throughly,
with admiration, when you were too much in love to take 155
notice of mine, which yet was but too visible. The name of
my family is Grey, my other Fidelia. The rest of my story
you shall know when I have fewer auditors.

MANLY

Nay, now, madam, you have taken from me all power of
making you any compliment on my part; for I was going to 160
tell you that for your sake only I would quit the unknown
pleasure of a retirement, and rather stay in this ill world of
ours still, though odious to me, than give you more frights
again at sea, and make again too great a venture there in
you alone. But if I should tell you now all this, and that your 165
virtue (since greater than I thought any was in the world)
had now reconciled me to't, my friend here would say 'tis
your estate that has made me friends with the world.

FREEMAN

I must confess I should, for I think most of our quarrels to
the world are just such as we have to a handsome woman: 170
only because we cannot enjoy her as we would do.

MANLY

Nay, if thou art a plain dealer too, give me thy hand, for now

153 *pretenders* suitors
154 *throughly* thoroughly

I'll say I am thy friend indeed; and for your two sakes,
though I have been so lately deceived in friends of both sexes,

> I will believe there are now in the world   175
> Good-natured friends who are not prostitutes,
> And handsome women worthy to be friends.
> Yet, for my sake, let no one e'er confide
> In tears or oaths, in love or friend untried.

(Exeunt omnes)

FINIS

EPILOGUE

Spoken by the WIDOW BLACKACRE

To you, the judges learned in stage laws,
Our poet now, by me, submits his cause;
For with young judges, such as most of you,
The men by women best their business do:
And truth on't is, if you did not sit here   5
To keep for us a term throughout the year,
We could not live by'r tongues; nay, but for you,
Our chamber-practice would be little too.
And 'tis not only the stage practiser
Who by your meeting gets her living here;   10
For as in Hall of Westminster
Sleek sempstress vents amidst the courts her ware,
So, while we bawl and you in judgment sit,
The visor-mask sells linen too i'th' pit.
O many of your friends, besides us here,   15
Do live by putting off their several ware.
Here's daily done the great affair o'th' nation;
Let love and us then ne'er have long vacation.
But hold; like other pleaders, I have done
Not my poor client's business, but my own.   20
Spare me a word then, now, for him. First know,
Squires of the long robe, he does humbly show
He has a just right in abusing you,
Because he is a brother-Templar too;

---

 8 *chamber-practice double entendre* referring to the work of a cham-
   ber-council, who does not plead in court
11 *Hall of Westminster* where Ned Ward saw sempstresses 'pleating
   Turn-overs and *Ruffles* for the *Young Students,* and Coaxing them
   with their *Amorous Looks, Obliging Cant,* and *Inviting Gestures,* to
   give so Extravagant a Price for what they Buy, that they may now
   and then afford to fling them a Nights Lodging into the Bargain'
   (*The London Spy,* ed. Ralph Straus (1924), p. 191)
12 *vents* sells
14 *visor-mask* the identifying disguise of a whore plying for custom in
   the pit
16 *putting off* selling, with a suggestion of fraud
24 *brother-Templar* Wycherley was admitted to the Inner Temple on
   10 November 1659.

For at the bar you rally one another,   **25**
And 'fool' and 'knave' is swallowed from a brother;
If not the poet here, the Templar spare,
And maul him when you catch him at the bar.
From you, our common modish censurers,
Your favour, not your judgment, 'tis he fears;   **30**
Of all loves begs you then to rail, find fault, ⎫
For plays, like women, by the world are thought, ⎬
When you speak kindly of 'em, very naught.   ⎭

26 *And 'fool'* Q1, 0 (Nay, fool Q2–8)